Caramel

CAROLE BLOOM

Photographs by ALEXANDRA DEFURIO

GIBBS SMITH
TO ENRICH AND INSPIRE HUMANKIND

First Edition
13 14 15 16 17   5 4 3 2 1

Text © 2013 Carole Bloom, CCP
Photographs © 2013 Alexandra DeFurio

Published by
Gibbs Smith
P.O. Box 667
Layton, Utah 84041

1.800.835.4993 orders
www.gibbs-smith.com

Designed by Rita Sowins / Sowins Design
Food styling by Anni Daulter, Delicious Gratitude

Printed and bound in Hong Kong
Gibbs Smith books are printed on paper produced from sustainable PEFC-certified
forest/controlled wood source. Learn more at www.pefc.org.

Library of Congress Cataloging-in-Publication Data

Bloom, Carole.
Caramel / Carole Bloom ; photographs by Alexandra DeFurio. — First edition.
pages cm
Includes index.
ISBN 978-1-4236-3212-2
1. Cooking (Caramel) 2. Desserts. I. DeFurio, Alexandra. II. Title.
TX767.C37B56 2013
641.6—dc23
2013001389

Other Books by Carole Bloom:
Intensely Chocolate / Bite-Size Desserts / The Essential Baker
Truffles, Candies, and Confections / All About Chocolate
Sugar & Spice / The International Dictionary of Desserts, Pastries, and Confections
The Candy Cookbook / Cookies for Dummies
Chocolate Lover's Cookbook for Dummies

To my boys:

My husband, Jerry, who is my rock;
Casanova, aka Mr. Handsome, our beautiful
silver tabby cat; and to the memory of Tiger,
aka Cutie Pie Boy, aka Peanut, our caramel-
colored tabby (Casanova's brother). They
make my life sweet and rich.

Contents

ACKNOWLEDGEMENTS

With thanks to:
My husband, Jerry who helps with everything
—ideas, tasting, buying ingredients, washing
dishes, and much more, including making me
laugh.

My agent, Susan Ginsburg, who is kind, caring,
easy to work with, and a true professional in
her field.

My editor, Michelle Branson, who was always
there for guidance and support, Alexandra
DeFurio for the gorgeous photographs and
Anni Daulter of Delicious Gratitude for creative
food styling, as well as Rita Sowins of Sowins
Design for the exciting book design.

My tasters, who include my Sunday yoga
friends, my husband's surfer friends, other
friends, and several neighbors for their very
supportive tasting reviews. People always ask
me what happens to everything that I make and
I tell them that I have a great group of friends
and neighbors who are the recipients of many
plates of goodies.

Art Pollard of Amano Artisan Chocolate for
his generosity in providing me with his excellent
chocolate to use for recipe testing. And Cory
Fields of Grand-Place Chocolate, Kate Hollis
of Taza Chocolate, and Rob Kopf of TCHO for
their chocolate.

Introduction

I HAVE WANTED TO CREATE A DESSERT COOKBOOK WITH ALL CARAMEL RECIPES FOR AS LONG AS I CAN REMEMBER. Not only is caramel a wonderful flavor on its own, but it goes so well with many other flavors. And caramel is not just for candies. Cakes, custards, tarts, ice creams, and many other desserts are taken to new and fantastic heights with the wonderful flavor of caramel.

Describing the flavor of caramel is not easy because caramel itself is often used to describe the flavors of other foods and beverages, like chocolate and wine. I think of caramel as having a mildly sweet flavor that is sweet and rich but not overpowering. Caramel likes to be right up front so you taste its flavor instantly. Caramel also prefers to linger, leaving a wonderful aftertaste. And caramel goes very well with just about everything in the dessert kitchen. Personally, I love caramel with chocolate and nut desserts. And I think everyone would agree that caramel has a wonderful aroma. Whenever I smell caramel, my taste buds perk right up in anticipation of something fabulous to come.

Food historians believe caramel is primarily an American creation. But as far back as AD 1000, Arab cultures were using something called *kurat al milh* which means small ball of sugar. This was made by crystallizing sugar in boiling water resulting in a sweet, firm, and crunchy substance. And it was the Arabs that created the first industrial sugar refinery on the island of Crete. It is believed that the English word "candy" came from the Arab word *qandi* which means crystallized sugar. In the late 1400s, Queen Elizabeth I enjoyed rock candy which is made by crystallizing sugar. By the late 1700s, the Dutch were making something called stroopwafels which used a caramel syrup filling. In the 1800s, the French and British worked to refine caramel, but it was the American, Milton Hershey, who, in 1883, established the Lancaster Caramel Company. Throughout the 1900s, caramel became part of the American sweet diet mostly in combination candy bars like the Snickers bar.

All of recipes in this book have been developed for home cooks. Although you might find similar caramel desserts in the best restaurants and pastry shops, I have designed these recipes for everyday home cooks. A very broad assortment of caramel dessert recipes is included in *Caramel*. This includes cakes, cupcakes, brownies, pies, tarts, cookies, candies, ice creams, and other caramel desserts.

Most of the ingredients and equipment used for the recipes in this cookbook may already be in your kitchen. But if they are not, they are all very easy to locate. You will find some basic techniques for working with caramel in the Caramel Techniques and Component Recipes chapter (pages 29–37). Here you will see that the process of caramelization is very easy and quick.

When you decide upon a caramel treat you want to try, be sure to read through the entire recipe before getting started to make sure you have all of the necessary equipment, utensils, and ingredients. I recommend you layout everything you will need; that way you will be prepared to make your recipe. If some preparation work is required, like chopping nuts, it's good to do this before actually starting to make your dessert. Also, some recipes require that a component part be made, such as Classic Caramel Sauce (page 33). If that is the case, it is best to make the necessary component part in advance. Of course, it is fine to reference the Utensils and Equipment (pages 21–27) and Caramel Techniques and Component Recipes (pages 29–37) chapters at any time.

I often have former students, friends, and family contact me asking for suggestions for desserts. Their question usually goes something like this: "I am not sure what to make because I don't know what they like." My answer is always: "Make a caramel dessert, you can't go wrong." I then go into a discussion about how easy it is to make caramel desserts and how there are so many dessert options.

Caramel is a flavor that most of us have grown up with and closely associate with the wowwee feeling of "that tastes so amazing!" The flavor of caramel is easily associated with creating a feeling of warmth and comfort. *Caramel* offers fresh and exciting caramel desserts that take this amazing and satisfying flavor to new heights. This book offers home cooks an easy way to make scrumptious caramel desserts that I am sure will become part of your home dessert repertoire to be enjoyed often by your friends and family.

Ingredients

THE NUMBER ONE RULE FOR INGREDIENTS IS TO USE THE BEST QUALITY YOU CAN. The freshest and purest, with no artificial anything, is preferred. Always check for expiration dates on new purchases and on goods that you have stored. It's best to have a well-stocked pantry for most often used ingredients. And storing ingredients in easy to access containers and jars is a good idea. Also, double checking to make sure everything is on hand for a recipe and premeasuring out all the required ingredients will make your caramel desserts even more fun to make.

✳ BUTTER ✳

Unsalted butter is used in all of my recipes because different brands of butter contain different amounts of salt. Using unsalted butter allows you control of the amount of salt that goes into recipes. For accuracy, I like to weigh the butter. Two tablespoons equal one ounce by weight. When a recipe calls for softened butter, the butter should be soft enough to hold the indentation of a finger but not so soft that it becomes liquid. I don't recommend substituting margarine or vegetable shortening for butter. They don't taste like butter and they work differently, so they won't produce the same flavor or texture as butter.

✳ DAIRY PRODUCTS ✳

Several different dairy products are used in the recipes in this cookbook, including cream cheese, crème fraîche, heavy whipping cream, mascarpone, milk, sour cream, and sweetened condensed milk. Each of these products brings its own special flavor and texture to the recipes. Always check the sell-by date on the carton to make sure you are buying a product that is as fresh as possible. It's best to store all dairy products in the refrigerator.

✳ EGGS ✳

Eggs are one of the main ingredients used in baking and have many roles, including providing flavor, texture, structure, leavening, moisture, and color. All of the recipes in this book use large eggs. Always check the date on the carton of eggs and buy them as fresh as possible. Do not use egg substitutes instead of real eggs.

✳ FLOUR ✳

Flour is a building block for making desserts, providing color, structure, and texture. Both all-purpose flour and cake flour are used in the recipes in this book. All-purpose flour is a blend of both hard and soft wheat that results in flour with a medium amount of protein, called gluten. Cake flour has less protein than all-purpose flour and is used to create a more delicate texture. Don't use bread flour which has much more protein than all-purpose flour and will create desserts that are tough and coarse grained. Also, don't use whole-wheat flour because it is dense and heavy.

If you want to make a recipe that calls for cake flour but you only have all-purpose flour, you can substitute the all-purpose flour. Just take out 2 tablespoons of all-purpose flour from each cup. Alternatively, if you want to replace cake flour for all-purpose flour, simply add 2 tablespoons of cake flour to each cup. The best way to measure flour is to fill a dry measuring cup then level it off at the top by moving a straight edge across the top.

✳ SALT ✳

Salt enhances the flavor of many ingredients used in desserts. I prefer to use either coarse kosher salt or fine-grained sea salt. These are both less salty than table salt and have a more delicate flavor. There is a wide variety of types and colors of sea salt available. Be sure to use sea salt that has a delicate flavor.

⁕ SUGAR ⁕

Sugar is an essential ingredient, especially for caramel. Sugar adds flavor, texture, moisture, and color to desserts. The recipes in this book use a variety of sugars, including granulated, superfine, confectioners', light and dark brown sugar, turbinado, and Demerara. Superfine sugar is sometimes sold as baker's sugar. It's more finely ground than granulated sugar and dissolves quickly, but one can be substituted for the other. Confectioners' sugar is also called powdered sugar. It is used to create a delicate texture in some dough and often for decorating. It can be lumpy and needs to be sifted before use.

Light and dark brown sugar contain more molasses than granulated sugar, giving them deeper flavor and a softer texture. Dark brown sugar has more molasses than light brown so its flavor is more intense. Brown sugar also has more moisture and air than other sugars. Because of this, it needs to be tightly packed into the measuring cup to get an accurate measure. Turbinado and Demerara are raw brown sugars with coarse crystals used mainly for garnishing, but they can be substituted for brown sugar. Store all sugars at room temperature in tightly sealed containers.

⁕ CHOCOLATE ⁕

Bittersweet chocolate, milk chocolate, and cocoa powder are used in some of the recipes in this book. Bittersweet chocolate (sometimes referred to as dark chocolate) has deep, rich chocolate flavor. I prefer to use bittersweet chocolate that has a cacao content between 64 and 72 percent. If you use chocolate that has more cacao content than 72 percent, it reacts differently with the other ingredients. For milk chocolate, I prefer to use dark milk chocolate that has a cacao content between 38 and 42 percent rather than standard milk chocolate that has between 10 and 12 percent cacao content. Either natural or Dutch-processed cocoa powder can be used with these recipes. Natural cocoa powder, which is light in color, has acidity and fruity qualities that are softened with alkali added during processing to make Dutch-processed cocoa, which also darkens the color.

✻ NUTS ✻

Several types of nuts are used in the recipes, including almonds, cashews, hazelnuts, macadamia nuts, pecans, peanuts, pistachio nuts, and walnuts. Buy nuts in the form you need them: sliced, slivered, ground, raw, salted, or unsalted. Nuts have a high content of natural oil that can go rancid. Because of this, it's best to buy them in small quantities that you will use quickly. Also, I recommend storing all nuts in the freezer.

Utensils & Equipment

AS WITH INGREDIENTS, HIGH QUALITY, TOP BRAND UTENSILS AND EQUIPMENT ARE RECOMMENDED. There are many products to choose from so watch for ones that have lifetime warranties as well as a good reputation for durability and reliability. Make sure equipment fits in your work area comfortably, pots and pans fit your stovetop and oven, and hand tools feel good in your hands. Sizes are important, so have on hand all the right sizes for everything, and maybe double up on some items that you use often. Storing utensils and equipment so they are easy to reach really helps streamline recipe making. Dishwasher safe products are great, if available. Keep in mind that utensils and equipment are a lifetime investment that will absolutely help to assure many years of great caramel desserts.

✳ BAKING SHEETS ✳

Baking sheets, also called jelly-roll pans, have several uses including baking cookies, scones, and holding tart, tartlet, pie, cake, and cupcake pans as they bake. Heavy aluminum baking sheets are the best to use because they don't buckle from the heat. These have 1-inch-high, straight-rolled rims on all sides. Baking sheets come in different sizes so be sure to purchase the size that fits in your oven and leaves at least 2 inches on all sides for air to circulate.

✳ BAKING, CAKE, TART, TARTLET, AND PIE PANS ✳

A large variety of shapes and sizes of cake and baking pans are used in the recipes in this book. Eight-inch square pans are made of aluminum. They have straight sides and are 2 inches deep. An angel food cake pan has straight sides with a center tube that helps conduct heat to the center of the cake as it bakes. It is 4 inches deep and made of heavy aluminum. A Bundt tube pan is a special deep cake pan with a center tube and deeply grooved rounded sides that form a pattern which is imprinted on the cake. Springform cake pans are made of aluminum and measure $9^1/_2$ x 3 inches. Round cake pans made of aluminum measure 9 inches in diameter and 2 inches deep. They have straight sides with no seams. A loaf cake pan that measures 9 x 5 x 3 inches is used for baking cakes in a loaf shape. This pan has straight sides. A standard aluminum cupcake pan with 12 cavities is used for baking cupcakes. Glass baking pans that measure 7 x 10 inches and 9 x 13 inches are used for baking bread pudding, some cookie recipes, and toffee. Silicone mini-muffin pans with 12 cavities that are each 2 inches round are used for some recipes. For tarts, use $9^1/_2$-inch-round fluted-edge pans with a removable bottom. Tartlets are baked in $2^1/_2$-inch-round fluted-edge tartlet pans. A 10-inch deep-dish pie pan is also used.

✳ CANDY THERMOMETER ✳

This is a vital tool when cooking sugar mixtures to a particular temperature. A candy thermometer reads between the range of 100 degrees F and 400 degrees F in two-degree increments. It's important that the thermometer takes the temperature of the mixture in the pan, not the bottom of the pan. Use a candy thermometer that has a metal body with a foot that sits on the bottom of the pan. Accuracy is extremely important because erring a few degrees in either direction can cause problems. For this reason, test the thermometer by placing it into a pan of boiling water and check that it reads 212 degrees F.

✳ FOOD PROCESSOR ✳

This is one of the most important pieces of equipment in the dessert kitchen. It easily makes tart and cookie dough and is excellent for chopping and grinding nuts. An extra bowl and blade are very handy to have.

✳ MEASURING CUPS AND SPOONS ✳

There are two different types of measuring cups, one for liquids and another for dry ingredients. Liquid measuring cups have a pour spout and a little extra room at the top for the liquid to move around without spilling. Dry measuring cups are available in nested sets of graduated sizes of $^1/_4$ cup, $^1/_3$ cup, $^1/_2$ cup, and 1 cup. Fill the dry measuring cup with the ingredient and level it off at the top using the straight edge of a knife or spatula. Measuring spoons are used for both liquid and dry ingredients. They usually come in sets of $^1/_4$ teaspoon, $^1/_2$ teaspoon, 1 teaspoon, and 1 tablespoon. Detaching them from the ring that holds them together as a set makes them easy to use. Having more than one set is also handy and allows you to move through a recipe without having to stop and clean up as you go.

✳ MIXER ✳

An electric mixer is another of the most important pieces of equipment in the dessert kitchen. A stand mixer allows your hands to be free to add ingredients or to attend to other tasks while it is mixing. Either a stand mixer or a hand-held mixer can be used to make the recipes in this book. If you have a stand mixer, I recommend keeping it on the countertop so it's easy to access. Also, having an extra bowl, flat beater, and wire-whip attachment lets you accomplish more without having to stop and tidy up.

✳ NONSTICK LINER ✳

These are made of silicone and can be re-used over and over again. They can't be cut to fit, but they are available in a variety of sizes, so buy the sizes that fit your pans.

✳ PARCHMENT PAPER ✳

This is greaseproof and nonstick. It is used primarily to line baking sheets and cake pans to keep cookies, scones, and cakes from sticking. When parchment paper is used, it is not necessary to butter and flour the pans. Parchment paper is also used to roll out pastry dough.

❋ PASTRY BRUSH ❋

Pastry brushes have several uses in the dessert kitchen, including washing down the sides of the pan while sugar mixtures are cooking. They are also used for brushing the tops of scones with liquid, buttering the inside of pans, and brushing excess flour off dough. I recommend natural bristle pastry brushes because they are softer than other materials and won't tear dough. One-inch-wide pastry brushes are the right size for most tasks. It's a good idea to keep brushes used for butter separate from those used to wash down the sides of pans. Pastry brushes with wooden handles should be washed by hand with hot, soapy water and not in the dishwasher, which will destroy the wooden handles over time.

❋ RAMEKINS, CUSTARD CUPS, AND BOWLS ❋

Some recipes call for $^1/_2$-cup size ramekins, custard cups, or bowls. These need to be heat safe because they are usually placed in the oven. Glass or ceramic are the best materials to use. Ramekins, custard cups, and bowls are available with either straight or flared sides. Either of these can be used as long as they hold the correct amount.

❋ ROLLING PIN ❋

A rolling pin is used to roll out dough for cookies, tarts, tartlets, and pies. Rolling pins are made from a variety of materials including wood, metal, glass, and silicone covered. Which type you choose is personal preference. The most important factor is that is feels comfortable in your hands.

❋ SAUCEPANS ❋

A variety of sizes of saucepans are used for the recipes in this book including 1-quart, 2-quart, and 3-quart. Because they are subject to high heat, these saucepans need to be heavy-duty. Enameled cast iron and heavy aluminum work very well and can take the heat. Pans made of copper are ideal for cooking sugar because they conduct the heat so quickly, but they are not required. Saucepans with a pour spout are more convenient to use for hot liquids.

✳ SCALE ✳

A reliable kitchen scale comes in very handy for accurately weighing chocolate and butter. There are a variety of types of scales available. I prefer an electronic scale that can be set to zero when a bowl is placed on top because it is extremely reliable. Keep the scale on the kitchen counter where it is easy to reach.

✳ SPATULAS ✳

Both rubber and heat-resistant spatulas have several uses in the dessert kitchen, such as stirring mixtures as they cook or melt, mixing and folding ingredients together, and scraping down the sides of mixing bowls. Keep silicone spatulas, which are heat safe, separate from rubber spatulas, which are not. Silicone spatulas come in a wide variety of colors, which is a good way to tell them apart from others. There are different sizes of spatulas; small, medium, and large. It's handy to have a few of each size. Straight and offset metal spatulas are very useful for spreading fillings, smoothing mixtures, releasing cookies from parchment paper, and for moving cakes and tarts to serving plates.

✳ TIMER ✳

An accurate timer is invaluable for knowing when your baked desserts are ready. Buy one that is easy to read and to use. Set the timer for the least amount of time called for in the recipe; you can always add more time, if needed. Also, a timer that allows for multiple timings are good to use in case there are several things that need to be watched. When I leave the kitchen while something is in the oven, I always take the timer with me so I can hear it ring.

classic
CARAMEL

Caramel
Techniques &
Component Recipes

CARAMEL is best defined as a flavor. It's a unique sweet, nutty, and toasty flavor that has a hint of maple and rum. This flavor is primarily obtained by cooking sugar. Granulated white sugar is most often used to achieve caramel flavor, however, light and dark brown sugars are also used. Cooked sweetened condensed milk, coconut milk, and white chocolate can also be used to obtain caramel flavor. Note that the flavor of caramel can take on different flavor profiles depending on the sugar, type of milk, cacao percentage of white chocolate, and time it is cooked. In addition, most caramel will have a slight vanilla flavor because vanilla is often used in caramel candies and desserts.

Caramelization is the process of cooking sugar until it reaches the flavor you desire. For granulated white sugar, there are three stages of caramelization that are determined by the color of the cooked sugar. These are light, medium, and dark. The darker the color the more pronounced the flavor. For this cookbook I use medium stage, which is amber in color. With light brown and dark brown sugars, caramel flavor is achieved during the heating or baking of the dessert. For condensed milk and coconut milk, caramel flavor is attained by cooking the milks to a thickened state and they are light brown in color. White chocolate caramelization occurs by baking small pieces until they are melted and tan in color. It is the milk solids in the white chocolate that allows for caramelization that creates the caramel flavor.

BUTTERSCOTCH is in the caramel family. It is often mistaken for caramel because it tastes similar but it usually has a more intense sweetness and buttery flavor. It is made similarly to caramel, as described above, but only light or dark brown sugars are used as well as butter. Butterscotch flavor is obtained by cooking the sugar or during the baking process.

TOFFEE is another caramel family member that is primarily a candy. Like butterscotch, the flavor of toffee is intensely sweet, although it has a slight bitterness. When making toffee, white sugar, light or dark brown sugar, and butter can be used, but the sugar is cooked to a very high temperature. This is what causes the slightly bitter, almost burnt taste.

BRITTLE is a distant relative of caramel. Like toffee, it mostly fits into the candy category. The flavor of brittle on its own is simply sugar sweet. But because brittle is usually used as a base for other ingredients, such as nuts, it is the other ingredients that mostly standout. Brittle is made with granulated white sugar and water (and other flavor ingredients) that are cooked to a high temperature then poured out onto a surface to harden.

✳ CARAMEL COOKING TIPS ✳

* To prevent burning, always cook the mixtures in a heavy-duty pan that heats evenly.
* It is best to use a larger pan than you think you will need when making a recipe that calls for adding liquid to the caramel because it bubbles up furiously.
* When adding cream or butter to hot caramel, be very careful because the mixture will bubble and foam. Always use a long-handle heat-resistant spatula and wear oven mitts.
* While cooking sugar, it is a good idea to wash down the sides of the pan a couple of times with a damp pastry brush. This prevents the sugar from crystallizing by pushing any stray crystals back into the mixture.
* Positively do not stir sugar mixtures as they cook. Stirring will cause the sugar to crystallize. It's fine to tilt the pan from side to side to even out the color as it cooks.
* Watch caramel closely as it cooks. It can go from clear blonde to dark very rapidly.
* Make sure the pan and utensils used are completely clean because foreign matter can cause sugar to crystallize.

The easiest way to clean the pan after cooking caramel is to fill it with water and bring it to a boil then let it cool somewhat before scrubbing it clean.

Classic Caramel Sauce

Makes 1 cup

You will be surprised at how quick and easy it is to make real homemade caramel sauce. Monitoring the heat and constantly stirring when adding in the cream and butter will give you just the right consistency, as well as a to-die-for caramel flavor.

3/4 cup heavy whipping cream
1/2 cup (3 1/2 ounces) granulated sugar
2 tablespoons water
1 teaspoon honey
4 tablespoons (2 ounces, 1/2 stick) unsalted butter, softened
1/2 teaspoon pure vanilla extract

Bring the cream to a boil in a 1-quart saucepan over medium heat.

Cook the sugar, water, and honey in a 3-quart heavy-duty saucepan over high heat until the mixture comes to a boil. Brush around the inside of the pan with a damp pastry brush at the point where the sugar syrup meets the sides of the pan. Do this twice during the cooking process to prevent the sugar from crystallizing. Cook the mixture over high heat, without stirring, until it turns amber colored, 6–8 minutes.

Lower the heat to medium and slowly add the hot cream to the sugar mixture while stirring constantly. The cream will bubble and foam. Continue stirring to make sure there are no lumps. Remove the saucepan from the heat and stir in the butter until it is completely melted. Then stir in the vanilla.

Transfer the caramel sauce to a bowl, cover tightly with plastic wrap, cool slightly, and serve warm.

KEEPING: Store the caramel sauce in a covered container in the refrigerator for up to 2 weeks. Cautiously warm in a microwave oven or in the top of a double boiler until fluid before using.

Dulce de Leche

Makes 1 1/3 cups

Dulce de Leche is made by cooking sweetened condensed milk until it thickens and caramelizes. It has a slight sweet cream flavor. It is very easy to make Dulce de Leche, but it's good to plan ahead because baking and cooling time can be nearly two hours.

1 can (14 ounces) sweetened condensed milk

Position a rack in the center of the oven and preheat to 425 degrees F.

Place the milk in an 8-inch square baking pan or a pie pan. Cover the pan tightly with aluminum foil and place the pan into a larger baking or roasting pan. Pour hot water halfway up the outsides of the baking pan or pie pan.

Bake until the mixture is thick and caramel brown, about 1 1/4 hours to 1 1/2 hours. Maintain the level of water in the larger pan by adding more water, if necessary, as the milk bakes.

Remove the baking pan from the water bath, uncover the pan, and place it on a wire rack to cool completely. When cool, cover the Dulce de Leche tightly with plastic wrap and chill in the refrigerator. Bring to room temperature before using.

KEEPING: Store the Dulce de Leche in a tightly covered container in the refrigerator for up to 4 days.

Caramelized White Chocolate

Makes 1 cup

This unusual recipe comes from L'Ecole du Grand Chocolat Valrhona in France. White chocolate is delicate, so be sure to keep the heat low. Also, to prevent any chance of the chocolate seizing, make sure all utensils are completely dry. This makes a delectable ingredient that adds its special flavor to other desserts.

12 ounces white chocolate, finely chopped
1/4 teaspoon kosher or fine-grained sea salt

Position a rack to the center of the oven and preheat to 250 degrees F.

Spread the chocolate onto a rimmed baking sheet and heat in the oven for 10 minutes. Remove the baking sheet from the oven and use a dry heat-resistant spatula to stir and spread the chocolate.

Return the baking sheet to the oven and bake for another 40–50 minutes, stirring every 10 minutes, until the chocolate is a deep golden color.

Remove the baking sheet from the oven, sprinkle the salt over the chocolate, and stir to distribute it evenly. If the chocolate is grainy or lumpy, pulse it in a food processor fitted with the steel blade for 1–2 minutes or smooth it with an immersion blender. The mixture should be fluid.

Transfer the caramelized white chocolate to a tightly covered container and store at room temperature in a cool, dry place. The chocolate will firm up at room temperature. To bring it back to a fluid texture, warm it in a microwave oven on low power for 30 second bursts or in the top of a double boiler over hot water.

KEEPING: Store in a tightly covered container, at room temperature, up to 2 months.

MAKING A CHANGE: To make caramelized milk chocolate; replace the white chocolate with the same amount of milk chocolate and proceed as instructed.

Praline

Makes about 2 cups

This mixture of caramelized nuts is chopped or finely ground, depending on its use. It adds extra flavor and texture to desserts. Any type of nuts can be used. Try sprinkling it over the top of ice cream or adding it to a pound cake, cupcakes, or brownies.

1 cup (7 ounces) granulated sugar
1/4 cup water
1/4 teaspoon cream of tartar
1 cup (4 1/2 ounces) whole or coarsely chopped toasted unsalted nuts

Line a baking sheet with a nonstick silicone mat.

Combine the sugar, water, and cream of tartar in a 2-quart heavy-duty saucepan. When the mixture begins to boil, brush around the inside of the pan with a damp pastry brush at the point where the sugar syrup meets the sides of the pan. Do this twice during the cooking process to prevent the sugar from crystallizing. Cook over high heat, without stirring, until it is a medium caramel color, about 9 minutes.

Add the nuts and stir with a heat-resistant spatula to coat them completely with the caramel. Remove the pan from the heat, pour the mixture onto the silicone mat on the baking sheet, and spread it out with the spatula. Work quickly because the mixture sets up rapidly.

Let the nut mixture cool completely, about 30 minutes, then break it into pieces with your hands. Place the pieces in the work bowl of a food processor fitted with the steel blade and pulse to chop the pieces to a medium-coarse consistency.

KEEPING: Store the praline in a tightly covered container, at room temperature, for up to 1 week or freeze in a freezer-safe container for up to 3 months.

Cakes, Cupcakes & Brownies

Butterscotch Pecan Bundt Cake

Makes 1 (10-inch) round cake, 12 to 16 servings

Both light and dark brown sugars are used to make this intensely flavored dense cake. The chopped pecans add even more flavor depth as well as a fresh crunchy texture. And to take this cake over the top, it is garnished with Classic Caramel Sauce. I like to use a nonstick Bundt cake pan to assure the baked cake releases easily. Also, use a serrated knife to cut the cake so that you can easily cut through the chopped pecans. Thin slices are definitely fine for this full-flavored cake.

Special equipment: 1 (10-inch) round Bundt pan

1$^1/_2$ cups (6 ounces) coarsely chopped pecans
Nonstick baking spray
16 tablespoons (8 ounces, 2 sticks) unsalted butter, softened
2 cups (12 ounces) firmly packed light brown sugar
1 cup (6 ounces) firmly packed dark brown sugar
$^1/_2$ cup canola or safflower oil
5 large eggs, room temperature
3 cups (13$^1/_2$ ounces) all-purpose flour
$^1/_2$ teaspoon baking powder
$^1/_2$ teaspoon kosher or fine-grained sea salt
1 cup milk (whole or 2%)
1 teaspoon pure vanilla extract
1 recipe Classic Caramel Sauce (page 33)

Position a rack in the center of the oven and preheat to 350 degrees F. Place the pecans in a cake or pie pan and toast for 8–10 minutes. Remove the pan from the oven and cool on a rack. Reduce the oven temperature to 325 degrees F. Spray the inside of the Bundt pan with nonstick baking spray.

Beat the butter in the bowl of an electric stand mixer using the flat beater attachment, or in a large bowl using a hand-held mixer, until fluffy, about 2 minutes. Add the sugars and beat together until completely blended.

Add the oil and blend together thoroughly. Add the eggs, 1 at a time, beating well after each addition.

continued

In a large bowl, sift together the flour and baking powder. Add the salt and toss to blend. Add this mixture to the butter mixture, alternating with the milk, in 4 stages, blending well after each addition. Stop occasionally and scrape down the bottom and sides of the bowl to ensure even mixing. Blend in the vanilla and the toasted pecans. Transfer the batter to the prepared Bundt pan.

Bake for 1 hour and 20 minutes, or until a cake tester inserted in the center comes out clean. Remove the pan from the oven and cool completely on a rack.

Invert the cake onto a serving plate, carefully lifting off the pan. Serve slices of the cake, at room temperature, garnished with a spoonful of caramel sauce.

KEEPING: The cake will keep tightly wrapped in aluminum foil, at room temperature, for up to 3 days.

ADDING STYLE: Serve slices of the cake with a scoop of Caramel Crunch Ice Cream (page 192).

Brown Sugar Toasted-Coconut Angel Food Cake (with Caramel Sauce)

Makes 1 (10-inch) round cake, 12 to 16 servings

Many angel food cakes have only a hint of flavor but that is definitely not the case with this one. Dark brown sugar combined with toasted coconut make an extraordinarily flavorful cake that is taken to the ultimate level with Classic Caramel Sauce and a sprinkle of toasted coconut as a garnish. It helps to use a serrated knife to slice the cake.

Special equipment: 1 (10-inch) round tube or Bundt pan

1¼ cups (2¼ ounces) sweetened shredded coconut

1 cup (4½ ounces) cake flour

⅛ teaspoon kosher or fine-grained sea salt

1½ cups (9 ounces) firmly packed dark brown sugar

¼ cup (1½ ounces) superfine sugar

12 large egg whites, room temperature

1 teaspoon cream of tartar

2 teaspoons pure vanilla extract

1 recipe Classic Caramel Sauce (page 33)

Position a rack in the center of the oven and preheat to 350 degrees F.

Place the coconut in a cake or pie pan and toast for 12 minutes, stirring every 3 minutes. Remove the pan from the oven and cool on a rack. Reduce the oven temperature to 325 degrees F.

In a medium bowl, sift the cake flour. Add salt and 1 cup of the toasted coconut and toss to blend.

Mix together the sugars in a small bowl. Whip the egg whites in the grease-free bowl of an electric stand mixer using the wire whip attachment, or in a large grease-free bowl using a hand-held mixer on medium speed, until frothy. Add the cream of tartar and continue to whip the egg whites. Very slowly sprinkle in the sugar until the egg whites hold glossy and firm, but not stiff peaks, about 5 minutes.

continued

Add the vanilla and blend in thoroughly. Remove the bowl from the mixer. Use a long-handle rubber spatula to fold the dry ingredients into the egg whites, in 4–5 stages.

Transfer the batter to the pan. Use a spatula to smooth and even the top then gently tap the pan on the countertop to eliminate any air bubbles. Bake for 40 minutes, or until a cake tester inserted in the center comes out clean. Remove the pan from the oven and invert it over a cooling rack onto its feet or hang it by the center tube over a funnel. Don't set the pan on the cooling rack or it will collapse as it cools. Leave the cake to cool completely. It should drop out of the pan on its own. If not, use a very thin bladed knife to run around the inner edge of the pan to help the cake release.

Serve slices of the cake, at room temperature, with a spoonful of caramel sauce. Sprinkle some of the remaining toasted coconut over each slice.

KEEPING: Store the cake tightly wrapped in plastic wrap for up to 3 days at room temperature. To freeze for up to 4 months, wrap the cake tightly in several layers of plastic wrap and aluminum foil. Label and date the package. If frozen, defrost overnight in the refrigerator and bring to room temperature before serving.

MAKING A CHANGE: Replace the toasted coconut with finely chopped walnuts or pecans.

Chocolate and Caramel Layer Cake

Makes: 1 (9-inch) round cake, 12 to 16 servings

If you are looking for a special occasion cake, this is it. Unsweetened chocolate along with light brown sugar and sour cream make up the basis for these dense, full-flavored cake layers. Caramel-Honey Whipped Cream is used for the filling and the cake is garnished with a light dusting of cocoa powder. To better assure even proportions when slicing the layers, rotate the cake as you slowly cut through it. When handling the cut layers, gently place your entire hand under the layer to prevent it from breaking.

Special equipment: 2 (9 x 2-inch) round cake pans

TO PREPARE THE CAKE PANS

1 tablespoon unsalted butter, melted and slightly cooled

1 tablespoon all-purpose flour

FILLING

2 recipes Caramel-Honey Whipped Cream (page 210)

CAKE

6 ounces unsweetened chocolate, finely chopped

1 3/4 cups (7 3/4 ounces) cake flour

1 teaspoon baking soda

1/2 teaspoon kosher or fine-grained sea salt

8 tablespoons (4 ounces, 1 stick) unsalted butter, softened

1 cup (6 1/2 ounces) superfine sugar

2/3 cup (4 ounces) firmly packed light brown sugar

2 large eggs, room temperature

1 tablespoon pure vanilla extract

1 cup sour cream or crème fraîche

1 teaspoon cocoa powder

Prepare the cream for Caramel-Honey Whipped Cream according to the recipe and chill for at least 3 hours.

continued

Position a rack in the center of the oven and preheat to 350 degrees F. Using a paper towel or a pastry brush, butter the inside of cake pans. Dust the inside of each pan with the flour. Shake and tilt the pans to cover the inside completely then turn the pans over and shake out the excess over the sink. Cut a round of parchment paper to fit the bottom of each pan. Butter each parchment paper round and place 1 in each pan, butter side up.

CAKE: Melt the chocolate in the top of a double boiler over low heat. Stir often with a rubber spatula to help melt evenly. Or melt the chocolate in a microwave oven on low power for 30 second bursts. Stir with a rubber spatula after each burst to help melt evenly.

In a small bowl, sift together the cake flour and baking soda. Add the salt and toss to blend.

Beat the butter in the bowl of an electric stand mixer using the flat beater attachment, or in a large bowl using a hand-held mixer on medium speed, until light and fluffy, about 2 minutes. Add the sugars to the butter and blend together well on medium speed. Stop occasionally and scrape down the sides and bottom of the bowl with a rubber spatula.

Using a fork, lightly beat the eggs with the vanilla in a small bowl. Add to the butter mixture. Mix together, stopping a few times to scrape down the sides and bottom of the mixing bowl. At first the mixture may look curdled, but as you stop and scrape down the bowl, the mixture will smooth out.

Alternately add the dry ingredients and the sour cream, in 4 stages, mixing well after each addition. Start with the dry ingredients and end with the sour cream. Stop after each addition and scrape down the bottom and sides of the bowl with a rubber spatula to help mix the ingredients together uniformly. Add the melted chocolate to the mixture and blend together thoroughly.

Divide the batter evenly between the cake pans. Smooth the top of each pan with a rubber spatula. Bake for 30–35 minutes, or until a cake tester inserted in the center comes out clean.

Remove the cake pans from the oven and cool completely on racks. Invert the pans to remove the layers then peel the parchment paper off the back of each layer. Re-invert the layers onto plates or cardboard cake circles.

FILLING: Whip the caramel cream with the honey in the bowl of an electric stand mixer using the wire whip attachment, or in a mixing bowl using a hand-held mixer, until the mixture holds soft peaks.

Using a long serrated knife, cut each cake layer in half horizontally. Place the bottom of 1 cake layer on a serving plate. Use an 8-inch flexible blade spatula to spread 1/4 of the whipped cream evenly over the cake layer, taking the cream just to the edges. Position the second cake layer evenly over the whipped cream and spread another 1/4 of the cream over it. Repeat with the remaining 2 cake layers and whipped cream. Lightly dust the top of the cake with cocoa powder before serving.

KEEPING: Store the cake loosely covered with aluminum foil in the refrigerator for up to 2 days.

STREAMLINING: Bake the cake layers up to 2 days before assembling the cake. After the layers are completely cool, cover them tightly with plastic wrap and hold at room temperature. The layers can be frozen for up to 3 months. To freeze, wrap them snugly in several layers of plastic wrap and place them into freezer bags. Label and date the package. If frozen, defrost the layers overnight in the refrigerator.

RECOVERING FROM A MISHAP: Don't worry if one of the cake layers breaks during assembly. You can patch it together with some of the whipped cream and no one will know the difference.

ADDING STYLE: If you would like to frost the cake, use Salted Caramel Buttercream Frosting (page 53). For added decoration, you can pipe the frosting through a pastry bag fitted with a star tip to cover the cake with buttercream stars.

Butterscotch Toasted-Walnut Pound Cake

Makes 1 (9 x 5 x 3-inch) loaf cake, about 10 servings

The butterscotch flavor of this dense cake comes from the mixture of dark brown sugar, butter, and cream. Toasted walnuts are a perfect match with butterscotch. You can slice this loaf cake thinner for more servings.

Special equipment: 1 (9 x 5 x 3-inch) loaf cake pan

Nonstick baking spray
1 1/4 cups (5 1/2 ounces) walnuts
2 cups (9 ounces) cake flour
1 teaspoon baking powder
1/4 teaspoon kosher or fine-grained sea salt
16 tablespoons (8 ounces, 2 sticks) unsalted butter, softened
1 cup (6 ounces) firmly packed dark brown sugar
4 extra-large eggs, room temperature
3 tablespoons heavy whipping cream
2 teaspoons pure vanilla extract

Line the loaf pan with aluminum foil, extending it slightly over the sides. Spray the foil with nonstick baking spray.

Position a rack in the center of the oven and preheat to 350 degrees F. Place the walnuts in a cake or pie pan and toast for 8 minutes. Remove the pan from the oven and cool on a rack then coarsely chop the walnuts. Reduce the oven temperature to 325 degrees F.

In a medium bowl, sift together the cake flour and baking powder. Add the salt and toss to blend well.

Beat the butter in the bowl of an electric stand mixer using the flat beater attachment, or in a large bowl using a hand-held mixer on medium speed, until fluffy, about 1 minute. Add the brown sugar and beat together well. Stop occasionally and scrape down the sides and bottom of the bowl with a rubber spatula.

Add the eggs, 1 at a time, to the butter mixture, blending well after each addition. The eggs may sit on top of the mixture, so stop after each addition and scrape down the sides of the bowl to mix evenly.

In a small bowl, combine the cream and vanilla. Add to the mixture, blending well. Add the flour mixture, in 3 stages, blending well after each addition. Then stir in the walnuts, blending completely.

Pour the cake batter into the prepared pan, smoothing the top with a rubber spatula. Bake for 1 hour and 10 minutes, or until the cake is light golden and a cake tester inserted near the center comes out clean. Remove the pan from the oven and cool completely on a rack. Grasp the foil to lift the cake from the pan then gently peel the foil away from the cake. Serve slices of the cake at room temperature.

KEEPING: Store the cake tightly covered in aluminum foil, at room temperature, for up to 4 days. To freeze for up to 3 months, wrap the cake tightly in several layers of plastic wrap and foil. Label and date the package. If frozen, defrost overnight in the refrigerator and bring to room temperature before serving.

MAKING A CHANGE: Replace the toasted walnuts with toasted pecans.

Chocolate Cupcakes with Salted Caramel Buttercream Frosting

Makes 24 cupcakes

These scrumptious cupcakes are made with unsweetened chocolate and are frosted with caramel buttercream that is made with Fleur de Sel sea salt. The caramel sauce used to flavor the buttercream can be made as long as a week in advance.

Special equipment: candy thermometer and 2 (12-cavity) muffin pans

CUPCAKES

6 ounces unsweetened chocolate, finely chopped

$1^3/_4$ cups ($7^3/_4$ ounces) cake flour

1 teaspoon baking soda

$^1/_2$ teaspoon kosher or fine-grained sea salt

8 tablespoons (4 ounces, 1 stick) unsalted butter, softened

1 cup ($6^1/_2$ ounces) superfine sugar

$^2/_3$ cups (4 ounces) firmly packed light brown sugar

2 large eggs, room temperature

1 teaspoon pure vanilla extract

2 teaspoons pure chocolate extract

1 cup sour cream

SALTED CARAMEL SAUCE

$^3/_4$ cup heavy whipping cream

1 cup ($6^1/_2$ ounces) granulated sugar

$^1/_4$ cup water

1 tablespoon light corn syrup

4 tablespoons (2 ounces, $^1/_2$ stick) unsalted butter, softened

$1^1/_2$ teaspoons pure vanilla extract

1 teaspoon Fleur de Sel salt

BUTTERCREAM FROSTING

2 large eggs, room temperature

2 large egg yolks, room temperature

$1^1/_2$ cups (10 ounces) granulated sugar, divided

$^1/_2$ cup water

$^1/_4$ teaspoon cream of tartar

16 tablespoons (8 ounces, 2 sticks) unsalted butter, softened

GARNISH

2 teaspoons Fleur de Sel or other fine finishing salt

Position the racks to the upper and lower thirds of the oven and preheat to 350 degrees F. Line the pans with cupcake papers.

continued

CUPCAKES: Melt the chocolate in the top of a double boiler over low heat, stirring often with a rubber spatula to help melt evenly. Or melt the chocolate in a microwave oven on low power for 30 second bursts. Stir with a rubber spatula after each burst to help melt evenly.

In a small bowl, sift the cake flour and baking soda together. Add the salt and toss to blend.

Beat the butter in the bowl of an electric stand mixer using the flat beater attachment, or in a large bowl using a hand-held mixer on medium speed, until light and fluffy, about 2 minutes. Add the sugars and beat together well on medium speed. Stop occasionally and scrape down the sides and bottom of the mixing bowl with a rubber spatula.

Using a fork, lightly beat the eggs with the vanilla and chocolate extracts in a small bowl. Add to the butter mixture and mix together, stopping a few times to scrape down the sides and bottom of the mixing bowl. At first the mixture may look curdled as the eggs are added, but as you stop and scrape down the bowl, the mixture will smooth out.

Alternately add the flour mixture and the sour cream, in 4–5 stages, mixing well after each addition. Stop after each addition and scrape down the bottom and sides of the bowl with a rubber spatula. Add the melted chocolate to the mixture and blend together thoroughly.

Use a 2-inch ice cream scoop to divide the batter evenly among the cavities in the pans. Bake the cupcakes for 8 minutes, switch the pans on the oven racks and bake another 8 minutes, until a cake tester inserted in the center comes out clean. Remove the pans from the oven and cool completely on racks.

SALTED CARAMEL SAUCE: Place the cream in a small saucepan and warm over medium heat until bubbles form at the edges.

While the cream is heating, combine the sugar, water, and corn syrup in a 2-quart heavy-duty saucepan. Cook over high heat, without stirring, until the mixture begins to boil. Brush around the inside of the pan with a damp pastry brush at the point where the sugar syrup meets the sides of the pan. Do this twice during the cooking process to prevent the sugar from crystallizing. Cook the mixture over high heat, without stirring, until it turns amber colored, about 10 minutes.

Stir in the hot cream using a long-handle heat-resistant spatula. Be very careful because it will bubble and foam. Stir to dissolve any lumps. Add the butter to the caramel mixture and stir until it is melted. Remove the saucepan from the heat and stir in the vanilla and salt. Transfer the caramel sauce to a container and cover tightly. Let the sauce cool then chill in the refrigerator until it is thick, about 2 hours.

BUTTERCREAM FROSTING: Whip the eggs, egg yolks, and ¼ cup of the sugar in the bowl of an electric stand mixer using the wire whip attachment, or in a large bowl using a hand-held mixer, until they are very pale colored and hold a slowly dissolving ribbon as the beater is lifted, about 5 minutes.

While the eggs are whipping, place the remaining sugar, water, and cream of tartar in a 2-quart heavy-duty saucepan. Bring the mixture to a boil, without stirring. Brush around the inside of the pan with a damp pastry brush at the point where the sugar syrup meets the sides of the pan. Do this twice during the cooking process to prevent the sugar from crystallizing. Cook over high heat, without stirring, until the mixture registers 242 degrees F on a candy thermometer (soft ball stage). Immediately remove the thermometer and place it in a glass of warm water then remove the pan from the heat so it won't continue to cook.

Adjust the mixer speed to low and pour the sugar syrup into the whipped eggs in a slow, steady stream. Aim the sugar syrup between the beater and the side of the bowl, so it doesn't get caught up in the beater or thrown against the sides of the bowl. Turn the mixer speed up to medium high and whip until the bowl is cool to the touch, about 8 minutes.

Adjust the mixer speed to medium and add the butter, 2 tablespoons at a time. Continue to beat until the mixture is thoroughly blended and fluffy. Add the cooled caramel sauce and stir until it is thoroughly blended.

Use a small spatula to frost the top of each cupcake with about 2 tablespoons of the frosting. You can also pipe the frosting onto the cupcakes in a decorative design. Sprinkle the top of each cupcake with a few grains of Fleur de Sel or other fine finishing salt. Serve the cupcakes at room temperature.

KEEPING: Store the unfrosted cupcakes tightly wrapped in aluminum foil for up to 3 days at room temperature. Store the frosted cupcakes in a single layer in an airtight plastic container in the refrigerator for up to 4 days. To freeze for up to 4 months, wrap the cakes tightly in several layers of plastic wrap and aluminum foil. Label and date the package. If frozen, defrost overnight in the refrigerator and bring to room temperature before serving.

MAKING A CHANGE: Add ⅔ cup toasted and coarsely chopped walnuts or pecans to the cupcake batter after adding the chocolate.

STREAMLINING: The caramel sauce can be prepared up to a week in advance and kept in a tightly covered container in the refrigerator. If it is too firm, soften it on low power in a microwave oven for 20 second bursts.

The Buttercream Frosting can be prepared up to 3 days in advance and kept in an airtight plastic container in the refrigerator or up to 4 months in the freezer. If frozen, defrost overnight in the refrigerator. To re-beat the Buttercream, break it up into chunks and place in a bowl. Place the bowl in a saucepan of warm water and let the Buttercream begin to melt around the bottom. Wipe the bottom of the bowl dry and beat the Buttercream with an electric mixer until it is fluffy and smooth.

Butterscotch Cupcakes with Dulce de Leche Frosting

Makes 16 cupcakes

You get double the pleasure with these yummy cupcakes. The smooth sweet Dulce de Leche Frosting goes perfectly with the butterscotch flavor of the cupcake. The frosting does not firm up like other frostings and the cupcake texture is light and slightly moist. You may want to make an extra batch of Dulce de Leche Frosting to have on hand for your next round of cupcakes.

Special equipment: 2 (12-cavity) cupcake pans

CUPCAKES

16 tablespoons (8 ounces, 2 sticks) unsalted butter, softened

1 1/2 cups (9 ounces) firmly packed dark brown sugar

2 large eggs, room temperature

2 large egg yolks, room temperature

1 teaspoon pure vanilla extract

2 1/4 cups (10 ounces) cake flour

2 teaspoons baking powder

1/2 teaspoon kosher or fine-grained sea salt

2/3 cup sour cream

DULCE DE LECHE FROSTING

16 tablespoons (8 ounces, 2 sticks) unsalted butter, softened

1 recipe Dulce de Leche (page 34)

Position the racks to the upper and lower thirds of the oven and preheat to 350 degrees F. Place each cupcake pan on a baking sheet. Line 16 cavities in the pans with cupcake papers. Place water in the remaining cavities, filling them 3/4 full.

CUPCAKES: Beat the butter in the bowl of an electric stand mixer with the flat beater attachment, or in a large bowl using a hand-held mixer on medium speed, until fluffy, about 2 minutes. Gradually add the brown sugar and beat the mixture until creamy, about 1 minute.

continued

Use a fork to lightly beat the eggs, egg yolks, and vanilla together in a small bowl. Add to the butter mixture, in 2 stages, beating well after each addition. Stop and scrape down the bottom and sides of the bowl with a rubber spatula. At first the mixture may look curdled, but as you stop and scrape down the bowl, the mixture will smooth out.

In a medium bowl, sift together the cake flour and baking powder. Add the salt and toss to blend. Add half of this mixture to the egg mixture and blend thoroughly. Add the sour cream and blend until smooth. Then add the remaining dry ingredients and blend thoroughly.

Use a 2-inch ice cream scoop to fill the cavities in the pans with the batter, dividing it evenly among them. Bake the cupcakes for 22 minutes, until light golden and a cake tester inserted in the center comes out clean.

Remove the pans from the oven and cool on racks. Pour the water out of the cupcake pan, then invert the pans to remove the cupcakes and turn them right side up.

DULCE DE LECHE FROSTING: Beat the butter in the bowl of an electric stand mixer using the flat beater attachment, or in a large bowl using a hand-held mixer, until soft and fluffy, about 2 minutes. Add the Dulce de Leche and blend together thoroughly.

Use a small offset spatula to spread the top of each cupcake with the frosting. If the frosting is too soft, chill the cupcakes for 15 minutes. You can also pipe the frosting onto the cupcakes in a decorative design. Serve the cupcakes at room temperature.

KEEPING: Store the unfrosted cupcakes tightly wrapped in aluminum foil for up to 3 days at room temperature. Store the frosted cupcakes in a single layer in an airtight plastic container in the refrigerator for up to 4 days. To freeze for up to 4 months, wrap the cakes tightly in several layers of plastic wrap and aluminum foil. Label and date the package. If frozen, defrost overnight in the refrigerator and bring to room temperature before serving.

MAKING A CHANGE: Frost the cupcakes with chilled Classic Caramel Sauce (page 33).

STREAMLINING: The frosting can be made up to 3 days in advance and kept in a tightly covered container in the refrigerator. Bring it to room temperature before using.

Caramelized Almond Financiers

Makes 12 Financiers

When I worked in Lausanne, Switzerland, at the Beau Rivage Palace Hotel, I made these classic French mini cakes often. Financiers (pronounced fee-nance-cee-airs) are traditionally made using almond flour, but with these Financiers, I use caramelized almond praline that is ground into a powder. This gives them a tasty caramel and roasted nutty flavor with a slightly moist texture. And there is a little crunchiness from the toasted sliced almonds that are sprinkled on the top. They are made in individual cupcake liners, making them great for on-the-go snacks and packed lunches.

Special equipment: 1 (12-cavity) 3-inch muffin pan

CARAMELIZED ALMOND PRALINE

1 cup (3 ounces) sliced almonds

1/2 cup (3 1/2 ounces) granulated sugar

2 tablespoons water

1/4 teaspoon cream of tartar

FINANCIERS

12 tablespoons (6 ounces, 1 1/2 sticks) unsalted butter

1 tablespoon pure vanilla extract or vanilla paste

4 large egg whites, room temperature

1/2 teaspoon cream of tartar

1 1/3 cups (4 1/2 ounces) confectioners' sugar, sifted

3/4 cup (3 1/4 ounces) all-purpose flour

Position a rack in the center of the oven and preheat to 350 degrees F. Line a jelly roll pan with a nonstick silicone mat.

CARAMELIZED ALMOND PRALINE: Place the almonds in a cake or pie pan and toast for 5–8 minutes, until light golden. Remove the pan from the oven and cool on a rack. Reserve 1/2 cup of the toasted almonds for the garnish.

Combine the sugar, water, and cream of tartar in a 2-quart heavy-duty saucepan. Cook over high heat, without stirring, until it is a medium caramel color, about 9 minutes. When the mixture begins to boil, brush around the inside of the pan with a damp pastry brush at the point where the sugar syrup meets the sides of the pan. Do this twice during the cooking process to prevent the sugar from crystallizing.

continued

Add $1/2$ cup of the almonds and stir with a heat-resistant spatula to coat them completely with the caramel. Remove the saucepan from the heat, pour the mixture onto the prepared pan, and spread it out with the spatula. Work quickly because the mixture sets up rapidly.

Let the almond mixture cool completely, about 30 minutes, then break it into pieces with your hands. Place the pieces in the work bowl of a food processor fitted with the steel blade and pulse to grind the pieces into a powder.

FINANCIERS: Line the cavities of the muffin pan with pleated paper muffin cups. Cut the butter into small pieces and place in a small saucepan with the vanilla. Cook over medium heat until the butter is foamy and light brown. Pour the mixture into a bowl and cool to lukewarm.

Whip the egg whites and cream of tartar in the bowl of an electric stand mixer using the wire whip attachment, or in a large mixing bowl using a hand-held mixer, on high speed until the egg whites hold soft peaks.

Slowly add the confectioners' sugar to the egg whites and continue whipping until they hold firm, glossy peaks.

Fold the flour into the egg whites, in 3 stages, blending thoroughly then fold in the ground caramelized almonds. Fold the cooled browned butter into the mixture, in 3 stages, blending thoroughly.

Use a $1^{1}/2$-inch ice cream scoop or a spoon to divide the batter evenly among the 12 muffin cups, filling each about $2/3$ full. Sprinkle the tops of the Financiers with the remaining $1/2$ cup almonds.

Bake the Financiers until they are light golden brown and a cake tester inserted in the center comes out clean, 12–15 minutes. Remove the pan from the oven and cool on a rack.

Serve the Financiers at room temperature.

KEEPING: Store the Financiers in an airtight plastic container between layers of waxed paper, at room temperature, for up to 3 days. To freeze for up to 2 months, wrap the container tightly in several layers of plastic wrap and aluminum foil. Label and date the package. If frozen, defrost overnight in the refrigerator and bring to room temperature before serving.

STREAMLINING: The praline can be made and stored in a tightly covered container, at room temperature, for up to 1 week. Or freeze in a freezer-safe container for up to 3 months.

Caramelized White Chocolate Hazelnut Mini Cakes

Makes 30 cakes

The blending of finely ground toasted hazelnuts and caramelized white chocolate makes these mini cakes very unique. This combination produces a rich flavor that has shades of dulce de leche. Their texture is dense and moist. The caramelized white chocolate can be made in advance and rewarmed in the microwave on low power or in the top of a double boiler over hot water. I like to bake the cakes in silicone mini-muffin pans because it's not necessary to line the pans and the cakes come out of the pans so easily. Serve two or three of these cuties with a scoop of Caramel Ice Cream (page 187).

Special equipment: 3 (12-cavity) 2-inch silicone mini-muffin pans

1¼ cups (6¼ ounces) whole raw hazelnuts

6 tablespoons granulated sugar, divided

¾ cup (3¼ ounces) all-purpose flour

½ teaspoon kosher or fine-grained sea salt

1½ cups Caramelized White Chocolate (page 35)

3 tablespoons (1½ ounces) unsalted butter, melted

4 large eggs, room temperature

Position a rack in the center of the oven and preheat to 350 degrees F. Place the hazelnuts on a rimmed baking sheet and toast for 15–18 minutes, until the skins split and the nuts turn golden brown. Remove the baking sheet from the oven and pour the nuts into a kitchen towel. Wrap the towel around the nuts and rub them together to remove most of the skins. Adjust the oven temperature to 375 degrees F and position the racks to the upper and lower thirds of the oven. Place the mini-muffin pans on baking sheets.

Pulse the hazelnuts and 3 tablespoons of sugar together in the work bowl of a food processor fitted with the steel blade until the nuts are finely ground, about 1 minute. Transfer the ground hazelnuts to a small bowl. Add the flour and salt and stir together until completely blended.

In a large bowl, stir together the Caramelized White Chocolate, butter, and remaining sugar. Stir in the eggs, 1 at a time, until well blended. Stir in the hazelnut mixture, in 3 stages, blending completely.

continued

Using an ice cream scoop or a spoon, scoop the mixture into 30 cavities of the mini-muffin pans, filling them to the top. Fill the remaining 6 cavities with water.

Bake the cakes for 7 minutes. Switch the baking sheets on the racks and bake another 7–8 minutes, until the cakes are firm at the outer edges but slightly soft inside.

Remove the baking sheets from the oven and transfer the mini-muffin pans to racks to cool completely. Invert the mini-muffin pans and the cakes will pop out then invert them so the tops are up. Serve the cakes at room temperature.

KEEPING: Store the cakes between layers of waxed paper tightly covered with aluminum foil, at room temperature, for up to 3 days.

STREAMLINING: The cake batter can be kept tightly covered in the refrigerator for up to 1 day before baking.

Caramel Pecan Cake Squares

Makes 16 (2-inch) squares

This moist caramel cake with toasted pecans is the quintessential comfort dessert. The squares are served with Classic Caramel Sauce, which takes them to the next level. For bite-size servings, these can be cut into 1-inch squares.

Special equipment: 1 (8-inch) square baking pan

1/2 cup (2 ounces) raw pecans
1 cup (6 1/2 ounces) granulated sugar
2/3 cup water, divided
1 large egg, room temperature
4 tablespoons (2 ounces, 1/2 stick) unsalted butter, melted
1/3 cup heavy whipping cream
1 1/4 cups (5 1/2 ounces) all-purpose flour
1/2 teaspoon baking soda
1/2 teaspoon kosher or fine-grained sea salt
1/2 cup (3 ounces) firmly packed dark brown sugar
Nonstick baking spray
1 recipe Classic Caramel Sauce (page 33)

Position a rack in the center of the oven and preheat to 350 degrees F. Place the pecans in a cake or pie pan and toast for 8 minutes. Remove the pan from the oven and cool on a rack then coarsely chop the pecans.

Combine the granulated sugar and 1/4 cup of the water in a 1-quart heavy-duty saucepan. When the mixture begins to boil, brush around the inside of the pan with a damp pastry brush at the point where the sugar syrup meets the sides of the pan. Do this twice during the cooking process to prevent the sugar from crystallizing. Cook over high heat, without stirring, until the mixture is a dark amber color, about 9 minutes. Carefully add the remaining water, stirring vigorously with a heat-resistant spatula. Be careful because the mixture will splatter. Keep stirring until the mixture is smooth. Remove from heat, transfer to a large bowl, cover with plastic wrap, and cool to room temperature.

In a small bowl, whisk or lightly beat the egg to break it up. Add the egg, butter, and cream to the bowl of caramel syrup, whisking to blend completely.

continued

In a large bowl, sift together the flour and baking soda. Add the salt and brown sugar and stir to blend well. Add the caramel mixture, whisking until smooth, then fold in the pecans. Cover the bowl and chill the mixture for 12–24 hours to firm the batter.

Position a rack in the center of the oven and preheat the oven to 325 degrees F. Line the baking pan with aluminum foil, extending it slightly over the sides. Spray the foil with nonstick baking spray. Turn the chilled cake batter into the prepared pan, smoothing the top with a rubber spatula. Bake for 35 minutes, until the top of the cake springs back when lightly touched. Remove the pan from the oven and cool completely on a rack. Grasp the foil to lift the cake from the pan then gently peel the foil away from the cake. Cut the cake into 4 (2-inch) rows in each direction, making 16 squares.

Serve the squares, at room temperature, drizzled with Classic Caramel Sauce.

KEEPING: Store the cake squares tightly covered in aluminum foil, at room temperature, for up to 4 days. To freeze for up to 3 months, wrap the cake squares tightly in several layers of plastic wrap and foil. Label and date the package. If frozen, defrost overnight in the refrigerator and bring to room temperature before serving.

MAKING A CHANGE: Replace the toasted pecans with toasted walnuts.

Caramel Swirl Cheesecake

Makes 1 (9¹⁄₂-inch) round cake, 12 to 16 servings

This cheesecake has Classic Caramel Sauce swirled into it, which makes it flavor-rich as well as visually exciting. The crust, made with toasted walnuts, provides a perfect balance of both flavor and texture. Because the cake needs time to cool and chill, I recommend making it at least a day in advance of when you plan to serve it.

Special equipment: 1 (9¹⁄₂-inch) round springform pan

CRUST

2 cups (9 ounces) walnuts

2 tablespoons firmly packed light brown sugar

4 tablespoons (2 ounces, ¹⁄₄ stick) unsalted butter, melted and cooled

CHEESECAKE

Nonstick baking spray

2 pounds cream cheese, room temperature

¹⁄₂ cup (3¹⁄₂ ounces) granulated sugar

¹⁄₂ cup (3 ounces) firmly packed light brown sugar

4 large eggs, room temperature

1 tablespoon pure vanilla extract

1¹⁄₂ cups sour cream

1 recipe Classic Caramel Sauce (page 33)

CRUST: Position a rack in the center of the oven and preheat to 350 degrees F. Place the walnuts in a cake or pie pan and toast for 12 minutes, stirring the pan after 6 minutes. Remove the pan from the oven and cool. Reduce the oven temperature to 300 degrees F.

Spray the inside of the springform pan with nonstick baking spray. Wrap heavy-duty aluminum foil tightly around the bottom of the pan to prevent water from seeping in as it bakes in a water bath.

Pulse the walnuts and brown sugar in the work bowl of a food processor fitted with the steel blade until the walnuts are finely ground, about 1 minute. Pour the butter through the feed tube and pulse until the mixture begins to hold together in moist clumps. Transfer the mixture to the springform pan and press the crust evenly onto the bottom.

continued

CHEESECAKE: Beat the cream cheese in the bowl of an electric stand mixer using the flat beater attachment, or in a large bowl using a hand-held mixer, until fluffy, about 2 minutes. Add the sugars and beat together well. Add the eggs, 1 at a time, beating well after each addition. Add the vanilla then add the sour cream and blend completely.

Pour ½ of batter into the prepared pan. Then pour ½ of the caramel sauce over the batter. Use the tip of a knife or a toothpick to swirl together. Repeat once more with the remaining batter and sauce.

Place the springform pan into a larger cake pan or a roasting pan. Pour boiling water into the bottom pan until it comes halfway up the sides of the cake pan. Bake the cake for 1 hour and 30 minutes, or until the cake puffs and the top is light golden. Remove the pans from the oven and transfer the springform pan to a cooling rack to cool completely. Cover the top of the cheese-cake with waxed paper and tightly wrap with aluminum foil then chill for at least 8 hours. Release the clip on the side of the spring-form pan and gently pull the sides away from the bottom.

Serve the cheesecake at room temperature.

KEEPING: Store the cake tightly wrapped in aluminum foil up to 4 days in the refrigerator. To freeze for up to 4 months, wrap the cake tightly in several layers of plastic wrap and foil. Label and date the package. If frozen, defrost overnight in the refrigerator and bring to room temperature before serving.

Dulce de Leche Milk Chocolate Cheesecake

Makes 1 (9 1/2-inch) round cheesecake, 12 to 16 servings

This cheesecake uses a unique flavor combination of milk chocolate and dulce de leche. The results are an extraordinarily rich and dense caramel milk chocolate flavor. It's surrounded by a crust of ground butter biscuits and walnuts and garnished with Classic Caramel Sauce. It's fine to cut small slices because this cheesecake is potently good. Be sure to make the cheesecake in advance because it needs time to cool and chill. It also freezes very well.

Special equipment: 1 (9 1/2-inch) round springform pan

COOKIE AND WALNUT CRUST

Nonstick baking spray

1 package (7 ounces) butter biscuits, wafers, or cookies

1 cup (4 1/2 ounces) walnuts

2 tablespoons light brown sugar

8 tablespoons (4 ounces, 1 stick) unsalted butter, melted and cooled

CHEESECAKE

14 ounces dark milk chocolate (38 to 42% cacao content), finely chopped

2 pounds cream cheese, softened

1/2 cup (3 1/2 ounces) granulated sugar

4 large eggs, room temperature

2 teaspoons pure vanilla extract

1/2 cup sour cream

1 recipe Dulce de Leche (page 34)

1 recipe Classic Caramel Sauce (page 33)

Position a rack in the center of the oven and preheat to 300 degrees F. Spray the inside of the springform pan with nonstick baking spray. Wrap heavy-duty aluminum foil tightly around the bottom of the pan to prevent water from seeping in as it bakes in a water bath.

COOKIE AND WALNUT CRUST: Pulse the cookies, walnuts, and brown sugar in the work bowl of a food processor fitted with the steel blade until the mixture is finely ground, about 2 minutes. Or place the cookies in a sturdy plastic bag and seal it. Use a rolling pin to crush the cookies to a very fine crumb consistency. Finely chop the walnuts and add them with the brown sugar to the cookies, seal the bag, and shake to blend together evenly.

Transfer the cookie mixture to a medium bowl and add the butter. Use a rubber spatula or a spoon to toss the mixture together to moisten all of the crumbs. Press the crumb mixture evenly into the bottom and most of the way up the sides of the springform pan.

CHEESECAKE: Melt the chocolate in the top of a double boiler over low heat. Stir often with a rubber spatula to help melt evenly. Remove the top pan of the double boiler and wipe the bottom and sides dry. Or place the chocolate in a microwave-safe bowl and melt on low power for 30 second bursts. Stir with a rubber spatula after each burst.

Beat the cream cheese in the bowl of an electric stand mixer using the flat beater attachment, or in a large bowl using a hand-held mixer, on medium speed until fluffy, about 2 minutes. Add the sugar and blend together very well. Stop occasionally and scrape down the sides and bottom of the bowl with a rubber spatula to ensure even blending.

Add the eggs, 1 at a time, to the cream cheese mixture, beating well after each addition. At first the eggs will sit on top of the cream cheese mixture, but stop often to scrape down the sides and bottom of the bowl with a rubber spatula. This will help the mixture to blend. The mixture may also look curdled, but will smooth out as you continue mixing.

Add the vanilla and sour cream to the mixture and stir together to combine well. Add the Dulce de Leche and mix together thoroughly. Then add the melted chocolate to the batter and mix together completely.

continued

Transfer the batter into the crust in the springform pan. Use a rubber spatula to smooth and even the top. Place the springform pan in a larger cake pan or roasting pan and set the pan on the oven rack. Carefully pour boiling water into the bottom pan until it reaches halfway up the side of the springform pan. Baking the cake in a water bath cushions it from the heat and adds extra moisture to the oven which keeps the top of the cake from cracking.

Bake the cake for 1 hour and 45 minutes, or until the top is set but jiggles slightly. Remove the pan from the oven and transfer the cheesecake to a rack. Remove the foil and let the cheesecake cool completely. Cover the top of the cheesecake with waxed paper and wrap the pan tightly with aluminum foil. Refrigerate the cake for at least 6 hours before serving.

Serve slices of the cake, at room temperature, with a spoonful of Classic Caramel Sauce drizzled over the top.

KEEPING: Store the cheesecake covered with waxed paper and tightly wrapped with aluminum foil in the refrigerator for up to 4 days. To freeze for up to 2 months, wrap the cake tightly in several layers of plastic wrap and aluminum foil. Label and date the package. If frozen, defrost overnight in the refrigerator and bring to room temperature at least 30 minutes before serving.

Caramel Swirl Brownies

Makes 16 brownies

Dark chocolate fans will love these rich brownies. The caramel mixture is drizzled and swirled on top of the brownie batter before baking. This not only creates an eye-catching design, but it offers a fabulous caramel and chocolate flavor sensation.

Special equipment: 1 (8-inch) square pan

CARAMEL

1/4 cup heavy whipping cream

1/4 cup (1 1/2 ounces) granulated sugar

1 tablespoon water

1 teaspoon light corn syrup

1 tablespoon (1/2 ounce) unsalted butter, softened

1/2 teaspoon pure vanilla extract

BROWNIES

1 tablespoon (1/2 ounce) unsalted butter, softened

4 ounces bittersweet chocolate (66% to 72% cacao content), finely chopped

2 ounces unsweetened chocolate, finely chopped

8 tablespoons (4 ounces, 1 stick) unsalted butter, cut into small pieces

1 teaspoon pure vanilla extract

1/4 teaspoon kosher or fine-grained sea salt

2 large eggs, room temperature

1/2 cup (3 1/2 ounces) granulated sugar

1/2 cup (3 1/2 ounces) firmly packed light brown sugar

1/2 cup (2 1/4 ounces) all-purpose flour

CARAMEL: Warm the cream in a small saucepan over medium-low heat until it forms bubbles around the edges. At the same time, combine the sugar, water, and corn syrup in a 1-quart heavy-duty saucepan and cook over high heat, without stirring. When the mixture begins to boil, brush around the inside of the pan with a damp pastry brush at the point where the sugar syrup meets the sides of the pan. Do this twice during the cooking process to prevent the sugar from crystallizing. Cook the mixture until it turns amber colored, about 5 minutes.

continued

Stir the hot cream into the caramel using a long-handle heat-resistant spatula. Be careful because the mixture will bubble and foam. Remove the pan from the heat and stir in the butter until it is completely melted. Stir in the vanilla. Transfer the caramel to a small bowl, cover tightly, and cool at room temperature while preparing the brownies.

BROWNIES: Position a rack in the center of the oven and preheat to 350 degrees F. Line the baking pan with aluminum foil that hangs over the sides. Use the tablespoon of butter to butter the inside of the foil.

Place both chocolates and the butter in the top of a double boiler over low heat. Stir often with a rubber spatula to help melt evenly. Remove the top pan of the double boiler and wipe the bottom and sides dry. Stir in the vanilla and salt thoroughly. Or place the chocolates and butter in a microwave-safe bowl and melt on low power for 30-second bursts. Stir with a rubber spatula after each burst to make sure it's melting. Let the mixture cool while mixing the rest of the batter, stirring with a rubber spatula occasionally to prevent a skin from forming on top.

Whip the eggs in the bowl of an electric stand mixer using the wire whip attachment, or in a large bowl using a hand-held mixer, until frothy, about 1 minute. Add the sugars and whip together on medium-high speed until the mixture is very thick and pale colored and holds a slowly dissolving ribbon as the beater is lifted, about 5 minutes.

Adjust the speed to low and add the chocolate mixture, blending completely. Stop and scrape down the sides and bottom of the bowl with the rubber spatula.

In 3 stages, add the flour to the batter, blending well after each addition. Stop and scrape down the sides and bottom of the bowl with a rubber spatula to help mix evenly.

Pour the batter into the prepared pan and use a rubber spatula to spread it evenly. Drizzle the caramel mixture over the top of the brownies in a random pattern. Use the point of a knife or a toothpick to draw through the caramel, creating a swirl design. Don't mix the caramel and the brownies together completely or it will lose the design as it bakes.

Bake for 30 minutes, or until a cake tester inserted in the center comes out with moist crumbs clinging to it. Remove the pan from the oven and cool completely on a rack.

Lift the brownies from the pan by holding the edges of the aluminum foil. Peel the foil away from the sides of the brownies and cut into 4 rows in each direction. Serve at room temperature.

KEEPING: Store the brownies between layers of waxed paper in an airtight plastic container, at room temperature, for up to 4 days. To freeze for up to 4 months, wrap the container tightly in several layers of plastic wrap and aluminum foil. Label and date the package. If frozen, defrost overnight in the refrigerator and bring to room temperature before serving.

MAKING A CHANGE: Add 1 cup toasted and coarsely chopped pecans to the brownie batter before turning it into the baking pan.

ADDING STYLE: Serve the brownies with Caramel Ice Cream (page 187).

Caramel-Layered Dark Chocolate Brownies

Makes 25 brownies

These intensely flavored dark chocolate brownies are spread with a layer of caramel then topped with bittersweet chocolate ganache. Caramel and deep chocolate flavor burst in your mouth with every bite. Both the brownies and the caramel can be made in advance then assembled the day you plan to serve them. Because these are so intense, a small square is extremely satisfying.

Special equipment: 1 (8-inch) square baking pan

BROWNIES

Nonstick baking spray

5 ounces unsweetened chocolate, finely chopped

2 ounces bittersweet chocolate, finely chopped

12 tablespoons (6 ounces, 1 1/2 sticks) unsalted butter, cut into small pieces

2 large eggs, room temperature

1 large egg yolk, room temperature

3/4 cup (5 ounces) superfine sugar

3/4 cup (4 1/2 ounces) firmly packed light brown sugar

1 teaspoon pure vanilla extract

3/4 cup (3 1/4 ounces) all-purpose flour

3 tablespoons natural cocoa powder

1/4 teaspoon kosher or fine-grained sea salt

CARAMEL

1 recipe Classic Caramel Sauce (page 33), chilled

BITTERSWEET CHOCOLATE GANACHE TOPPING

4 ounces bittersweet chocolate (64 to 72% cacao content), finely chopped

1/2 cup heavy whipping cream

BROWNIES: Position a rack in the center of the oven and preheat to 350 degrees F. Line the baking pan with aluminum foil, letting it hang about two inches over the sides. Coat the inside of the foil with nonstick baking spray.

continued

Place both chocolates and the butter together in the top of a double boiler over low heat. Stir often with a rubber spatula to help melt evenly. Remove the top pan of the double boiler and wipe the bottom and sides dry. Or place the chocolates and butter in a microwave-safe bowl and melt on low power for 30-second bursts. Stir with a rubber spatula after each burst to make sure it's melting. Let the mixture cool while mixing the rest of the brownie batter. Stir with a rubber spatula occasionally to prevent a skin from forming on top.

Whip the eggs and egg yolk in the bowl of an electric stand mixer using the wire whip attachment, or in a large bowl using a hand-held mixer, until frothy, about 1 minute.

Add the sugars to the eggs and whip together until the mixture is very thick and pale colored and holds a slowly dissolving ribbon as the beater is lifted, about 5 minutes. Add the vanilla and stir to blend well.

Add the chocolate mixture to the egg mixture and blend completely on low speed. Stop and scrape down the sides and bottom of the bowl with the rubber spatula. The mixture will be smooth and dark chocolate colored.

In a medium bowl, sift the flour and cocoa powder together. Add the salt and stir to combine.

In 3 stages, add the dry ingredients to the chocolate mixture, blending well after each addition. Stop and scrape down the sides and bottom of the bowl with a rubber spatula to help mix evenly.

Pour the batter into the prepared pan and use a rubber spatula to spread it evenly. Bake for 35 minutes, or until a cake tester inserted in the center comes out with slightly moist crumbs clinging to it. Remove the pan from the oven and cool completely on a rack.

CARAMEL: Stir the caramel sauce until it is smooth. Pour it onto the top of the cooled brownies and spread evenly into the corners using a small offset spatula. Chill in the freezer for 30 minutes to set the caramel.

BITTERSWEET CHOCOLATE GANACHE TOPPING: Place the chocolate in a medium bowl. Heat the cream in a small saucepan until bubbles form around the edges. Pour the cream over the chocolate and let stand for 30 seconds. Stir the cream and chocolate together with a heat-resistant spatula until completely melted and smooth.

Remove the pan of brownies from the freezer. Pour the ganache over the top of the caramel layer and spread it out evenly into the corners using a small offset spatula. Chill the brownies in the refrigerator for about 20 minutes to set the ganache.

Lift the brownies from the pan using the edges of the aluminum foil then peel the foil away from the brownies. Use a large knife to cut the brownies into 5 rows in each direction. Dip the knife in hot water and dry between cuts. Gently separate the brownies and serve at room temperature.

KEEPING: Store the brownies without the topping between layers of waxed paper in an airtight plastic container, at room temperature, for up to 4 days. To freeze for up to 4 months, wrap the container tightly in several layers of plastic wrap and aluminum foil. Label and date the package. If frozen, defrost overnight in the refrigerator and bring to room temperature before serving.

Store the brownies with the topping loosely covered with waxed paper and tightly covered with aluminum foil, at room temperature, for up to 3 days.

MAKING A CHANGE: Add 1 cup roughly chopped walnuts to the batter before pouring into the pan to bake and mix them in thoroughly.

STREAMLINING: The Classic Caramel Sauce can be made up to 2 weeks in advance and kept in a tightly covered container in the refrigerator.

Butterscotch Blondies

Makes 16 (3 x 2¹/₂-inch) triangles

Blondies are brownies that are made without chocolate. Adding praline helps boost the butterscotch flavor of these cake-like treats. These are usually served at room temperature, but they also can be warmed. They are great for breakfast or afternoon tea.

Special equipment: 1 (8-inch) square baking pan

Nonstick baking spray
8 tablespoons (4 ounces, 1 stick) unsalted butter, softened
1 cup (6 ounces) firmly packed dark brown sugar
2 large eggs, room temperature
2 teaspoons pure vanilla extract
1 cup (4¹/₂ ounces) all-purpose flour
¹/₄ teaspoon baking powder
¹/₄ teaspoon kosher or fine-grained sea salt
1 cup Praline (page 36) made with pecans

Position a rack in the center of the oven and preheat to 350 degrees F. Line the baking pan with aluminum foil, letting it hang about two inches over the sides. Spray the foil with nonstick baking spray.

Beat the butter in the bowl of an electric stand mixer using the flat beater attachment, or in a large bowl using a hand-held mixer, until fluffy, about 2 minutes. Add the brown sugar and blend thoroughly, about 2 minutes.

Use a fork to lightly beat together the eggs and vanilla in a small bowl. Add to the butter mixture and blend well. The mixture will look curdled but will smooth out when the dry ingredients are added.

In a medium bowl, mix together the flour, baking powder, and salt. In 3 stages, add the dry ingredients to the butter mixture, blending well after each addition. Scrape down the sides and bottom of the bowl with the rubber spatula.

Add the Praline and stir to blend well. Pour the mixture into the prepared pan and use a rubber spatula to spread it evenly into the corners.

Bake for 25–27 minutes, or until a cake tester inserted in the center comes out clean. Remove the pan from the oven and cool completely on a rack.

Lift the blondies from the pan with the aluminum foil. Carefully peel the foil away from the sides of the blondies. Cut into half horizontally and vertically, forming squares. Cut each square in half diagonally, forming triangles, then cut across the width of each triangle, forming 16 smaller triangles.

KEEPING: Store the blondies in an airtight container between layers of waxed paper, at room temperature, for up to 4 days. To freeze for up to 4 months, wrap the container tightly in several layers of plastic wrap and aluminum foil. Label and date the package. If frozen, defrost overnight in the refrigerator and bring to room temperature before serving.

ADDING STYLE: Serve the cooled blondies with a scoop of Caramel Ice Cream (page 187).

Tarts, Tartlets & a Pie

Caramel Cashew Tart

Makes 1 (9½-inch) round tart, 12 to 14 servings

This tart resembles a candy bar. Two layers of bittersweet chocolate ganache enclose a chewy mixture of caramel and toasted chopped cashews. This all rests on a delicate sweet pastry shell. There are a few steps involved in preparing this tart that can easily be spread out over a couple of days.

Special equipment: 1 (9½-inch) round, fluted-edge removable-bottom tart pan

PASTRY DOUGH

1¼ cups (5½ ounces) all-purpose flour

½ cup (1¾ ounces) confectioners' sugar

⅛ teaspoon kosher or fine-grained sea salt

8 tablespoons (4 ounces, 1 stick) unsalted butter, chilled

1 large egg yolk, room temperature

½ teaspoon pure vanilla extract

BITTERSWEET CHOCOLATE GANACHE

6 ounces bittersweet chocolate (66% to 72% cacao content), finely chopped

⅔ cup heavy whipping cream

CARAMEL CASHEW FILLING

¾ cup (5 ounces) granulated sugar

¼ cup water

1 tablespoon light corn syrup

⅓ cup heavy whipping cream

6 tablespoons (3 ounces, ¾ stick) unsalted butter, softened

½ teaspoon pure vanilla extract

Pinch of kosher or fine-grained sea salt

1½ cups (6¾ ounces) toasted cashews, coarsely chopped

GARNISH

20 cashew pieces

continued

PASTRY DOUGH: Briefly pulse together the flour, sugar, and salt in the work bowl of a food processor fitted with the steel blade. Cut the butter into small pieces and add. Pulse until the butter is cut into very tiny pieces, about 30 seconds. The texture will be sandy with very tiny lumps.

In a small bowl, use a fork to beat the egg yolk and vanilla together. With the food processor running, pour this mixture through the feed tube. Process until the dough wraps itself around the blade, about 1 minute. Shape the dough into a flat disk and wrap tightly in a double layer of plastic wrap. Chill in the refrigerator until firm before using, about 2 hours.

Position a rack in the center of the oven and preheat to 375 degrees F. On a smooth, flat surface, roll out the dough between sheets of lightly floured waxed or parchment paper to a large rectangle ¼ inch thick. Peel off the top piece of paper, brush off any excess flour, and gently roll the pastry dough around the rolling pin. Place the tart pan directly under the rolling pin and carefully unroll the dough into the pan. Gently lift up the edges and fit the dough against the bottom and sides of the tart pan, pushing it lightly into the fluted edges. Trim off any excess dough at the top edge of the pan and patch any places that have holes or tears. Place the pan on a baking sheet and freeze for 15 minutes.

Line the shell with a large piece of aluminum foil that fits well against the bottom and sides and fill with tart weights. Bake the shell for 10 minutes then remove the foil and weights. Lightly pierce the bottom of the shell with a fork to release air and prevent it from puffing up. Bake another 12–15 minutes, until light golden and set. Remove the baking sheet from the oven and transfer the tart pan to a rack to cool completely.

BITTERSWEET CHOCOLATE GANACHE: Place the chocolate in a large bowl. Heat the cream in a small saucepan until bubbles form around the edges. Pour the cream over the chocolate and let stand for 30 seconds. Stir the cream and chocolate together with a heat-resistant spatula until completely melted and smooth. Pour half of this mixture into the cooled tart shell. Cover the bowl with remaining ganache tightly with plastic wrap and hold at room temperature. Place the tart shell in the refrigerator to set the filling, 30–45 minutes.

CARAMEL CASHEW FILLING: Combine the sugar, water, and corn syrup in a 3-quart heavy-duty saucepan. Stir over medium-high heat to dissolve the sugar. Brush the sides of the pan with a pastry brush dipped in water and cook the mixture, without stirring, until it turns amber colored, about 8 minutes. At the same time heat the cream to a boil in a small saucepan.

When the caramel mixture turns amber, add the hot cream, butter, vanilla, and salt and stir constantly. Be careful because the mixture will bubble and foam. When the butter is completely melted, add the toasted cashews and stir to coat them completely with the caramel mixture. Pour the mixture into a large bowl and chill in the refrigerator until cool and spreadable, about 15 minutes.

Pour the caramel cashew filling over the chocolate ganache in the tart shell, spreading it evenly.

Warm the remaining chocolate ganache in a small saucepan over low heat or in a microwave-safe bowl on low power for 30 second bursts, stirring often, until the mixture is fluid. Pour the ganache over the caramel cashew filling and spread it out evenly.

GARNISH: Place the cashew pieces close together around the outer edges of the tart, or coarsely chop and sprinkle over the top. Chill the tart for 45 minutes to 1 hour, until firm, but not hard. Serve slices of the tart at room temperature.

KEEPING: Store the tart on a plate lightly covered with waxed paper then tightly wrapped in aluminum foil in the refrigerator for up to 3 days.

STREAMLINING: The pastry dough can be made up to 4 days in advance and kept tightly wrapped in plastic wrap in the refrigerator. To freeze for up to 3 months, place it in a freezer safe bag. Label and date the package. If frozen, defrost overnight in the refrigerator and bring to room temperature before using.

The pastry dough can be baked up to 2 days in advance and kept tightly wrapped in aluminum foil at room temperature.

MAKING A CHANGE: Replace the cashews with walnuts or pecans.

Caramel Coconut Tart

Makes 1 (9 1/2-inch) round tart, 12 to 14 servings

If you are a lover of coconut, this tart is for you. A sweet pastry shell with coconut is pre-baked and filled with a mixture of Classic Caramel Sauce and crème fraîche then topped with toasted coconut. The coconut and caramel flavors complement each other perfectly and the toasted coconut on top adds a delightful chewiness to this tart. Because the pastry shell is rather delicate, make sure to use an extra sharp knife and push all the way to the bottom to get clean slices.

Special equipment: 1 (9 1/2-inch) round, fluted-edge removable-bottom tart pan

PASTRY DOUGH

1 cup (4 1/2 ounces) all-purpose flour

1/3 cup (1 1/4 ounces) confectioners' sugar

3/4 cup (1 1/2 ounces) sweetened shredded coconut

1/8 teaspoon kosher or fine-grained sea salt

8 tablespoons (4 ounces, 1 stick) unsalted butter, chilled

1 large egg yolk, room temperature

1/2 teaspoon pure almond extract

GARNISH

1 cup (2 ounces) sweetened shredded coconut

CARAMEL FILLING

1/2 cup crème fraîche

1 recipe Classic Caramel Sauce (page 33), room temperature

PASTRY DOUGH: Briefly pulse together the flour, sugar, coconut, and salt in the work bowl of a food processor fitted with the steel blade. Cut the butter into small pieces and add. Pulse until the butter is cut into very tiny pieces, about 30 seconds. The texture will be sandy with very tiny lumps.

In a small bowl, use a fork to beat the egg yolk and almond extract together. With the food processor running, pour this mixture through the feed tube. Process until the dough wraps itself around the blade, about 1 minute. Shape the dough into a flat disk and wrap tightly in a double layer of plastic wrap. Chill in the refrigerator until firm before using, about 2 hours.

continued

Position a rack in the center of the oven and preheat to 375 degrees F. On a smooth, flat surface, roll out the pastry dough between sheets of lightly floured waxed or parchment paper to a large rectangle ¼ inch thick. Peel off the top piece of paper, brush off any excess flour, and gently roll the pastry dough around the rolling pin. Place the tart pan directly under the rolling pin and carefully unroll the dough into the pan. Gently lift up the edges lift up the sides and fit the dough against the bottom and sides of the tart pan, pushing it lightly into the fluted edges. Trim off any excess dough at the top edge of the pan and patch any places that have holes or tears. Place the pan on a baking sheet and freeze for 15 minutes.

Line the shell with a large piece of aluminum foil that fits well against the bottom and sides and fill with tart weights. Bake the shell for 12 minutes then remove the foil and weights. Lightly pierce the bottom of the shell with a fork to release air and prevent it from puffing up. Bake another 12–15 minutes, until light golden and set. Remove the baking sheet from the oven and transfer the tart pan to a rack to cool completely.

GARNISH: Reduce the oven temperature to 350 degrees F. Spread the coconut in a cake or pie pan and toast in the oven for 12–15 minutes, stirring after every 3 minutes, until the coconut is light golden. Remove the pan from the oven and cool completely on a rack.

CARAMEL FILLING: Place the crème fraîche in the bowl of an electric stand mixer or large bowl. Use the wire whip attachment or a hand-held mixer to whip the crème fraîche on medium speed until it holds soft peaks. In 3 stages, fold the whipped crème fraîche into the caramel sauce until thoroughly blended.

Transfer the filling to the tart shell and spread it evenly. Sprinkle the toasted coconut evenly over the top of the tart. Serve slices of the tart at room temperature.

KEEPING: Store the tart on a plate lightly covered with waxed paper then tightly wrapped in aluminum foil in the refrigerator for up to 3 days.

STREAMLINING: The pastry dough can be made up to 4 days in advance and kept tightly wrapped in plastic wrap in the refrigerator. To freeze for up to 3 months, place it in a freezer safe bag. Label and date the package. If frozen, defrost overnight in the refrigerator and bring to room temperature before using.

The pastry dough can be baked up to 2 days in advance and kept tightly wrapped in aluminum foil at room temperature.

Caramelized Walnut Tart

Makes 1(9$^{1}/_{2}$-inch) round tart, 12 to 14 servings

I learned to make this classic tart while visiting the mountainous Engadine region of Switzerland when I worked in Lausanne. Slices of the tart are easy to carry in your pack when hiking. And it stays moist, holds its shape, and provides energy. But you don't have to be a hiker to enjoy this. It's a perfect fall and winter dessert.

Special Equipment: 1 (9$^{1}/_{2}$-inch) round, fluted-edge removable-bottom tart pan

PASTRY DOUGH

2$^{1}/_{2}$ cups (11$^{1}/_{4}$ ounces) all-purpose flour

$^{1}/_{3}$ cup (2 ounces) granulated sugar

$^{1}/_{8}$ teaspoon salt

16 tablespoons (8 ounces, 2 sticks) unsalted butter, chilled

1 large egg, room temperature

1 teaspoon pure vanilla extract

CARAMELIZED WALNUT FILLING

1$^{1}/_{4}$ cups (8 ounces) granulated sugar

$^{1}/_{4}$ cup water

$^{2}/_{3}$ cup heavy whipping cream

1 tablespoon honey

2 cups (9 ounces) walnuts, finely chopped

GARNISH

1 extra-large egg, room temperature

PASTRY DOUGH: Briefly pulse the flour, sugar, and salt in the work bowl of a food processor fitted with the steel blade. Cut the butter into small pieces and add. Pulse until the butter is cut into very tiny pieces, about 30 seconds. The texture will be sandy with very tiny lumps.

Use a fork to beat the egg and vanilla extract together in a small bowl. With the food processor running, pour this mixture through the feed tube. Process until the dough wraps itself around the blade, 30 seconds to a minute.

continued

Divide the pastry dough in half. Place each half onto a large piece of plastic wrap. Shape into a flat disk and wrap tightly in a double layer of plastic wrap. Chill in the refrigerator until firm before using, about 2 hours. Chilling the dough relaxes the gluten in the flour so it won't be too elastic and will roll out easily. It also firms up the butter in the dough so it will need less flour when rolled out. If the dough is too firm, it will splinter and break when rolled out. Let it stand at room temperature for 10–15 minutes to become more pliable.

Position a rack in the center of the oven and preheat to 425 degrees F.

On a smooth, flat surface, roll out half of the pastry dough between sheets of lightly floured waxed or parchment paper to a large circle about 11 inches in diameter. Carefully peel the paper off the top of the dough. Brush excess flour off of the dough then gently roll the dough around the rolling pin. Place the tart pan directly underneath the rolling pin and carefully unroll the dough onto it.

Gently lift up the sides and fit the pastry dough against the bottom and sides of the tart pan, pushing it lightly into the fluted edges. Trim off the excess dough by running the rolling pin over the top of the pan. Or use your fingers to press against the top of the pan to remove the excess dough.

CARAMELIZED WALNUT FILLING: Place the sugar and water in a 3-quart heavy-duty saucepan. Cook over high heat, without stirring, until the mixture begins to boil. Brush around the inside of the pan with a damp pastry brush at the point where the sugar syrup meets the sides of the pan. Do this twice during the cooking process to prevent the sugar from crystallizing. Cook the mixture over high heat, without stirring, until it turns amber colored, about 10 minutes.

At the same time, heat the cream in a small saucepan until it begins to boil. Pour the hot cream into the caramel mixture. Stir together using a long-handle wooden spoon or heat-resistant spatula. Be very careful because it will bubble and foam. Stir for a minute or two to dissolve any lumps.

Stir the honey into the caramel mixture then add the walnuts and stir to coat them completely. Quickly transfer the mixture to the tart shell and spread it out evenly.

On a smooth, flat surface, roll out the remaining half of pastry dough between sheets of lightly floured waxed or parchment paper to a large circle about 9½ inches in diameter. Carefully peel the paper off the top of the dough.

Brush the top edge of the bottom pastry shell lightly with water. Brush excess flour off of the dough then gently roll the pastry dough around the rolling pin. Place the tart pan directly underneath the rolling pin and carefully unroll the top piece of dough onto it. Press the pastry dough down so it will stick to the sides of the bottom dough and remove any excess dough.

Use a fork to pierce the top of the dough in several places to create steam holes and make a design.

GARNISH: Lightly beat the egg in a small bowl with a fork. Brush the top of the tart with the beaten egg 2 times.

Place the tart pan on a baking sheet and bake for 25 minutes, until the top is golden. Remove the baking pan from the oven and cool the tart on a rack.

Remove the sides of the tart pan before serving. Cut the tart into slices and serve at room temperature.

KEEPING: The tart can last for up to 3 days tightly wrapped with aluminum foil at room temperature.

STREAMLINING: The pastry dough can be made in advance and kept in the refrigerator, tightly wrapped in a double layer of plastic wrap, for up to 4 days. To freeze for up to 3 months, wrap the dough snugly in several layers of plastic wrap and place it into a freezer bag. Label and date the package. If frozen, defrost overnight in the refrigerator before using. The pastry dough can also be fit into the tart pan and kept tightly covered in the refrigerator or frozen, wrapped and labeled as above.

MAKING A CHANGE: Replace the walnuts with pecans or almonds. Replace half of the walnuts with almonds, cashews, or pecans.

Caramelized Upside-Down Pear Tart

Makes 1 (10-inch) round tart, 12 to 14 servings

The rewards of this tart make it well worth the extra steps to prepare. It's a variation of the classic French dessert, *Tarte Tatin*, but made with pears with just a hint of vanilla. Tender buttery pastry dough makes up the bottom of this tart. Make sure to flip the baked tart over quickly to avoid any of the filling spilling out. For cutting, use a serrated knife so that the pears cut cleanly.

Special equipment: 1 (10-inch) pie pan

PASTRY DOUGH

1 cup (4 1/2 ounces) all-purpose flour

1/4 teaspoon granulated sugar

1/8 teaspoon salt

6 tablespoons (3 ounces, 3/4 stick)
  unsalted butter, chilled

3 tablespoons cold water

CARAMEL

1/2 cup (3 1/2 ounces) granulated sugar

1/2 cup water

1/8 teaspoon cream of tartar

PEAR FILLING

2 pounds (5 to 6 medium) firm Bosc pears

4 tablespoons (2 ounces, 1/4 stick)
  unsalted butter

1/3 cup (2 ounces) granulated sugar

1 teaspoon pure vanilla extract

PASTRY DOUGH: Briefly pulse the flour, sugar, and salt in the work bowl of a food processor fitted with the steel blade. Cut the butter into small pieces and add. Pulse until the butter is cut into very tiny pieces, about 30 seconds. The texture will be sandy with tiny lumps.

With the food processor running, add the water through the feed tube. Process until the dough forms a ball around the blade, about 30 seconds. Form the dough into a flat disk and wrap tightly in a double layer of plastic wrap. Chill in the refrigerator until firm before using, about an hour.

CARAMEL: Place the sugar, water, and cream of tartar in a 1/2-quart heavy-duty saucepan. Bring the mixture to a boil over medium-high heat, without stirring. Brush around the inside of the pan with a damp pastry brush at

continued

the point where the sugar syrup meets the sides of the pan. Do this twice during the cooking process to prevent the sugar from crystallizing. Cook the mixture over high heat until it turns medium-caramel color.

Immediately remove the saucepan from the heat and pour the caramel into the bottom of the pie pan. Swirl the pan to completely coat the bottom with the caramel.

PEAR FILLING: Use a vegetable peeler or a knife to peel the pears then cut them into quarters. Remove the core from each quarter and cut them into 1/2-inch-thick lengthwise slices.

Heat the butter over medium heat in a 10-inch sauté pan until it is foamy. Add the pears and sprinkle them with sugar. Stir the pears to coat them with the sugar. Cook over medium heat until the pears are golden and soft, stirring often with a wooden spoon or heat-resistant spatula, about 15 minutes. Add the vanilla and stir to blend in well. Transfer the cooked pears to a parchment paper lined baking sheet to cool.

Position a rack in the lower third of the oven and preheat to 400 degrees F. On a smooth, flat work surface, roll out the pastry dough between sheets of lightly floured waxed or parchment paper to a 12-inch circle.

Arrange the cooled, cooked pear slices in tight concentric circles over the caramel in the pie pan.

Gently roll the pastry dough around the rolling pin and unroll over the pears. Or fold the dough in half, place on top of the pears, and unfold. Tuck the dough in so that the pears are completely covered. Pierce the dough in several places to release steam while it bakes.

Bake the tart for 45 minutes, until the pastry is golden and puffed. Remove the tart from the oven and cool on a rack for 15 minutes.

Place a serving plate over the pan and carefully invert the tart onto the plate. Gently lift the pan off of the tart. If any pear slices stick to the pan, use a spatula to carefully remove them and arrange on top of the tart.

Serve the tart warm, or at room temperature, with Caramel Ice Cream (page 187) or lightly sweetened whipped cream.

KEEPING: Although the tart is best eaten the day it's made, it can last for up to 2 days. Store the tart loosely covered with waxed paper then tightly wrapped with aluminum foil in the refrigerator. It can be rewarmed in a 350 degree F oven for 15 minutes.

STREAMLINING: The pastry dough can be rolled out in advance and kept in the refrigerator tightly wrapped in a double layer of plastic wrap for up to 3 days.

Caramel-Apricot Linzertorte

Makes 1 (9 1/2-inch) round tart, 12 servings

When the invitation goes out around my house for a special dessert, linzertorte is always near the top of the request list. Linzertorte is a classic Austrian pastry that comes from the town of Linz, which is located about midway between Vienna and Salzburg. I use the traditional buttery ground almond pastry dough for the shell and lattice topping, but instead of filling it only with preserves, I use a scrumptious blend of apricot preserves and Classic Caramel Sauce. If the pastry dough breaks when you are placing it in the tart pan or when making the lattice topping, simply patch it where necessary with a pinch from the excess dough. To get clean smooth servings, cut the slices with a serrated knife.

Special equipment: 1 (9 1/2-inch) round, fluted-edge removable-bottom tart pan

ALMOND PASTRY DOUGH

1 cup (4 1/2 ounces) all-purpose flour

1 1/2 cups (4 1/2 ounces) finely ground almonds

1/2 cup (3 1/2 ounces) granulated sugar

1 1/2 teaspoons ground cinnamon

1/4 teaspoon ground cloves

16 tablespoons (8 ounces, 2 sticks) unsalted butter, chilled

2 large egg yolks, room temperature

CARAMEL-APRICOT FILLING

1 cup Classic Caramel Sauce (page 33), chilled

1/4 cup apricot preserves

PASTRY DOUGH: Briefly pulse together the flour, almonds, sugar, cinnamon, and cloves in the work bowl of a food processor fitted with a steel blade. Cut the butter into small pieces and add to the mixture in the food processor. Pulse until the butter is cut into very tiny pieces, about 30 seconds.

Use a fork to lightly beat the egg yolks in a small bowl. With the food processor running, pour the egg yolks through the feed tube. Process the dough until the mixture wraps itself around the blade, about 1 minute. Shape the pastry dough into a flat disk and tightly wrap in a double layer of plastic wrap. Chill in the refrigerator until firm before using, 3–4 hours.

continued

Position a rack in the center of the oven and preheat to 375 degrees F. Cut off $\frac{1}{3}$ of the pastry dough and keep it chilled while working with the other portion. On a smooth, flat surface, roll out the pastry dough between sheets of lightly floured waxed or parchment paper to a large round, about 11 inches in diameter. Carefully peel the paper off the top of the dough. Gently roll the dough around the rolling pin. Place the tart pan directly underneath the rolling pin and carefully unroll the dough into the pan. Gently lift up the sides and fit the pastry dough against the bottom and sides of the tart pan. Trim off any excess dough at the top of the pan. Transfer the tart pan to a baking sheet.

CARAMEL-APRICOT FILLING: In a large bowl, whisk together the caramel sauce and apricot preserves. Spread the filling evenly on the pastry in the tart pan.

On a smooth, flat surface, roll out the remaining pastry dough between sheets of lightly floured waxed or parchment paper to a rectangle about 12 x 6 inches. Carefully peel the paper off the top of the dough. Use a fluted edge pastry wheel to cut $\frac{1}{2}$-inch-wide strips of the dough. Use a long-handle offset spatula to wedge underneath each strip of pastry dough and gently transfer it to the top of the linzertorte. Make a lattice by laying the strips in a woven pattern, first in one direction then in the other direction, alternating as they are placed.

Roll remaining dough into a long rope about $\frac{1}{4}$-inch thick. Place this around the top outer edge where the ends of the lattice strips meet the edge of the tart. Use a fork to press the rope into the edges of the tart and make a pressed design. Chill the linzertorte for 15 minutes before baking.

Position a rack in the center of the oven and preheat to 375 degrees F. Bake for 30 minutes, until the pastry is set and the filling is bubbling. Remove the pan from the oven and transfer the tart pan to a rack to cool completely.

Remove the sides of the tart pan and cut the linzertorte into 12 equal slices. Serve at room temperature.

KEEPING: Store the tart tightly wrapped in aluminum foil, at room temperature, for up to 3 days.

STREAMLINING: The pastry dough can be made up to 3 days in advance. To freeze for up to 3 months, place the wrapped pastry dough in a freezer bag. Label and date the package. If frozen, defrost it in the refrigerator before using.

TROUBLESHOOTING: Once the pastry dough is unrolled into the tart pan, don't push it down forcefully. This will stretch the dough, which will shrink as it bakes.

Caramelized Banana Turnovers

Makes 8 (6-inch) turnovers

These turnovers almost seem tropical. Light and flaky puff-pastry squares are filled with caramelized bananas, nutmeg, and vanilla. A caramel glaze is drizzled over the top of the turnovers, which gives them an extra flavor boost. Be careful not to overfill your puff-pastry squares because if your mixture seeps out during baking it will harden and burn on the baking pan. These are great any time of day and it is fine to reheat them, preferably in the oven.

Special equipment: 2 baking sheets

TURNOVERS

1 package store-bought puff pastry, defrosted

4 medium-size firm bananas

6 tablespoons (3 ounces, $^3/_4$ stick) unsalted butter, cut into small pieces

$^2/_3$ cup (4 ounces) firmly packed light brown sugar

1 teaspoon freshly grated nutmeg

1 teaspoon pure vanilla extract

1 large egg, room temperature

CARAMEL GLAZE

$^1/_2$ cup (3$^1/_2$ ounces) granulated sugar

$^1/_4$ cup water

$^1/_8$ teaspoon cream of tartar

TURNOVERS: Roll each piece of puff pastry out between sheets of lightly floured waxed paper to a 12-inch square. Use a ruler to cut each square into equal size quarters, making a total of 8 (6-inch) squares. Place the squares on parchment paper-lined baking sheets and chill while preparing the filling.

Peel each banana and slice in half lengthwise. Then cut each half into quarters across the width. Melt the butter in a 10-inch sauté pan over medium heat. When the butter begins to bubble, add the bananas.

Sprinkle the brown sugar, nutmeg, and vanilla over the bananas and stir until they are evenly coated. Cook the bananas, stirring often, until they are soft and caramelized, about 10 minutes. Transfer the bananas to a plate to cool slightly.

Position the oven racks to the upper and lower thirds of the oven and preheat to 425 degrees F.

Use a fork to lightly beat the egg in a small bowl. Use a pastry brush to brush the top edges of each square with beaten egg. Be sure to brush only the inner part of the dough, not the outside. This will help the pastry dough stick together when the turnovers are formed.

Place 2 heaping tablespoons of the banana filling in the center of each square. Bring opposite corners of the square together and fold each pastry square in half, lining up all the edges and points, making a triangle. Pinch the edges together firmly then crimp with a fork or roll the edges in slightly to give them a finished look. Place the turnovers on the lined baking sheets, leaving at least an inch of space between them.

Use a pastry brush to brush the top of each turnover with the beaten egg. Be careful that the egg doesn't run down the sides and underneath the turnovers. If it does, wipe it up because it can cause the bottom of the turnovers to burn.

Bake the turnovers for 8 minutes then switch the baking sheets on the racks and bake another 7 minutes. Switch the baking sheets again and bake another 8–12 minutes, until the turnovers are golden.

CARAMEL GLAZE: Place the sugar, water, and cream of tartar in a small saucepan and bring to a boil over high heat. Brush around the inside of the pan with a damp pastry brush at the point where the sugar syrup meets the sides of the pan. Do this twice during the cooking process to prevent the sugar from crystallizing. Cook the mixture over high heat, without stirring, until it turns amber colored, 6–8 minutes.

Drizzle the caramel over the turnovers. It will set quickly. Let the turnovers stand for about 20 minutes then use a small spatula to loosen them from the baking sheet. Serve the turnovers warm or at room temperature.

The turnovers can be rewarmed at 350 degrees F. To do this, place them in a single layer on a baking sheet lined with parchment paper and bake for 10–15 minutes.

KEEPING: Store the turnovers loosely covered with waxed paper then tightly wrapped with aluminum foil at room temperature for up to 2 days.

Caramel Mousse Chocolate Tartlets

Makes 16 (2^1/$_2$-inch) tartlets

The airy texture of the caramel mousse combined with the light and crunchy dark chocolate pastry shells is sure to excite anyone's taste buds. These can be served in a variety of creative ways, such as on a large decorative platter or individually on a cocktail napkin.

Special equipment: 32 (2^1/$_2$-inch) round, fluted-edge tartlet pans and
  1 (12-inch) pastry bag with a large open star tip

COCOA PASTRY DOUGH

1 cup (4^1/$_4$ ounces) all-purpose flour
^{1}/$_4$ cup (^{3}/$_4$ ounces) cocoa powder, natural or Dutch processed
^{1}/$_3$ cup (2 ounces) superfine sugar
^{1}/$_8$ teaspoon kosher or fine-grained sea salt
6 tablespoons (3 ounces, ^{3}/$_4$ stick) unsalted butter, chilled
1 large egg, room temperature
1 teaspoon pure vanilla extract

CARAMEL MOUSSE

1 cup heavy whipping cream, divided
^{1}/$_4$ cup (1^3/$_4$ ounces) granulated sugar
^{1}/$_4$ cup firmly packed (1^3/$_4$ ounces) light brown sugar
2 tablespoons water
1 teaspoon honey
^{1}/$_2$ teaspoon pure vanilla extract
2 tablespoons (1 ounce) unsalted butter, softened

COCOA PASTRY DOUGH: Briefly pulse the flour, cocoa powder, sugar, and salt in the work bowl of a food processor fitted with a steel blade. Cut the butter into small pieces and add. Pulse until the butter is cut into very tiny pieces, about 30 seconds. The texture will be sandy with very tiny lumps.

Use a fork to beat the egg and vanilla together in a small bowl. With the food processor running, pour this mixture through the feed tube. Process until the dough wraps itself around the blade, about 1 minute. Shape the dough into a flat disk and tightly wrap in a double layer of plastic wrap. Chill in the refrigerator until firm before using, about 2 hours.

Position a rack in the center of the oven and preheat to 350 degrees F. On a smooth, flat surface, roll out the pastry dough between sheets of lightly floured waxed or parchment paper to a large rectangle about ¼ inch thick. Peel off the top piece of paper and brush off any excess flour. Use a 3-inch-round plain-edge cutter to cut out circles of dough. Gently lift up a dough circle and fit it into the bottom and against the sides of a tartlet pan. Place another tartlet pan on top of the dough to act as a weight as they bake. Repeat with the remaining dough circles. Gather together any scraps, roll, cut, and fit into the tartlet pan. Place the tartlet pans on a baking sheet.

Bake the shells for 8 minutes. Remove the baking sheet from the oven, remove the top tartlet pans, and return the baking sheet to the oven. Bake the tartlet shells another 8 minutes, or until set. Remove the baking sheet from the oven and cool completely on a rack. Gently tap the tartlet pans against a countertop to help remove the tartlet shells. Place them on a serving plate and cover tightly with aluminum foil.

CARAMEL MOUSSE: Bring ⅓ cup of the cream to a boil in the small heavy-duty saucepan over medium heat. Cook the sugars, water, honey, and vanilla in a 2-quart heavy-duty saucepan over high heat until the mixture comes to a boil. Brush around the inside of the pan with a damp pastry brush at the point where the sugar syrup meets the sides of the pan. Do this twice during the cooking process to prevent the sugar from crystallizing. Cook the mixture over high heat, without stirring, until it turns amber colored, 6–8 minutes.

Lower the heat to medium and slowly add the hot cream to the sugar mixture while stirring constantly. The cream will bubble and foam. Continue to stir to make sure there are no lumps. Remove the saucepan from the heat and stir in the butter until it is completely melted. Transfer the caramel mixture to a medium bowl, cover tightly with plastic wrap, cool to room temperature, then chill until thick, about 2 hours.

Whip the remaining cream in the bowl of an electric stand mixer using the wire whip attachment, or in a large bowl using a hand-held mixer, until it holds soft peaks. Fold the whipped cream into the chilled caramel mixture, in 3 stages.

Fill the pastry bag partway with the mousse. Pipe mounds of the mousse into the tartlet shells, dividing it evenly among the shells. Or use a small ice cream scoop to place the mousse into the tartlet shells. Serve the tartlets at room temperature.

KEEPING: The dough can be frozen for up to 1 month and defrosted overnight in the refrigerator. Store the tartlets without the mousse filling tightly covered with aluminum foil, at room temperature, for up to 3 days. Store the filled tartlets in the refrigerator for 1 day.

Caramel-Filled Double Chocolate Tartlets

Makes 18 (2¹/₂-inch) tartlets

Intensely chocolate with oozing rich caramel is the best way to describe these tartlets. A delicate cocoa pastry shell is filled with Classic Caramel Sauce then topped off with a thick layer of Bittersweet Chocolate Ganache. The first taste sensation is chocolate, followed instantly by smooth, rich caramel. It is fine to use the tip of a small paring knife or pointed small metal spatula to help release the pastry shells from the tartlet molds. To protect the smooth ganache on top of the finished tartlets, do not allow anything to touch the surface of them.

Special equipment: 36 (2¹/₂-inch) round, fluted-edge tartlet pans

COCOA PASTRY DOUGH
1 recipe Cocoa Pastry Dough (page 102)

CARAMEL FILLING
1¹/₂ recipes Classic Caramel Sauce (page 33)

BITTERSWEET CHOCOLATE GANACHE
6 ounces bittersweet chocolate (66 to 72% cacao content), finely chopped
²/₃ cup heavy whipping cream

Position a rack in the center of the oven and preheat to 350 degrees F. On a smooth, flat surface, roll out the pastry dough between sheets of lightly floured waxed or parchment paper to a large rectangle about ¼ inch thick. Peel off the top piece of paper and brush off any excess flour. Use a 3-inch-round plain-edge cutter to cut out circles of dough. Gently lift up a dough circle and fit it into the bottom and against the sides of a tartlet pan. Plan another tartlet pan on top of the dough to act as a weight as they bake. Repeat with the remaining dough circles. Gather together any scraps, roll, cut, and fit into the tartlet pan. Place the tartlet pans on a baking sheet.

Bake the tartlet shells for 8 minutes. Remove the baking sheet from the oven, remove the top tartlet pans, and return the baking sheet to the oven. Bake the tartlet shells another 8 minutes, or until set. Remove the baking sheet from the oven and cool completely on a rack. Gently tap the tartlet pans against a countertop to help remove the tartlet shells. Place them on a serving plate and cover tightly with aluminum foil.

continued

CARAMEL FILLING: If the caramel sauce is firm, warm it until fluid in a microwave oven on low power or in the top of a double boiler over hot water. Use a 1½-inch ice cream scoop or a spoon to fill each pastry shell ¾ full. Let the caramel stand at room temperature until firm or chill in the refrigerator for 30 minutes.

BITTERSWEET CHOCOLATE GANACHE: Place the chocolate in a large bowl. Heat the cream in a small saucepan until bubbles form around the edges. Pour the cream over the chocolate and let stand for 30 seconds. Stir the cream and chocolate together with a heat-resistant spatula until completely melted and smooth. Use a 1½-inch ice cream scoop or a spoon to cover the top of each tartlet with ganache, dividing it evenly among the tartlets. Place the plate of tartlets in the refrigerator to set the chocolate, for 20 minutes.

Serve the tartlets at room temperature.

KEEPING: Store the tartlets covered with waxed paper then tightly wrapped with aluminum foil, at room temperature, for up to 3 days.

STREAMLINING: The tartlet shells can be baked up to 2 days before filling. Store them at room temperature tightly wrapped in aluminum foil.

Classic Caramel Sauce can be made up to a week in advance. Store it tightly covered in the refrigerator.

ADDING STYLE: Serve each tartlet with a scoop of Caramel Ice Cream (page 187) or Caramel Crunch Ice Cream (page 192).

Salted Peanut Caramel Tartlets

Makes 20 (2$^{1}/_{2}$-inch) round tartlets

These flavor-forward tartlets practically melt in your mouth. Delicate sweet pastry shells are filled with a gooey rich caramel mixture that has finely toasted, chopped, and salted peanuts. The peanuts provide just a slight amount of texture while adding even more flavor. To easily release the tartlets from the molds, insert the tip of a narrow thin-blade knife. These can be eaten as finger food, but remind your tasters not to squeeze too hard when they pick up the tartlet because the pastry shells will break.

Special equipment: 40 (2$^{1}/_{2}$-inch) round, fluted-edge tartlet pans

PASTRY DOUGH

1$^{1}/_{4}$ cups (5$^{1}/_{2}$ ounces) all-purpose flour

$^{1}/_{2}$ cup (1$^{3}/_{4}$ ounces) confectioners' sugar

$^{1}/_{8}$ teaspoon kosher or fine-grained sea salt

8 tablespoons (4 ounces, 1 stick) unsalted butter, chilled

1 large egg yolk, room temperature

$^{1}/_{2}$ teaspoon pure vanilla extract

SALTED PEANUT CARAMEL FILLING

1 cup heavy whipping cream

$^{1}/_{2}$ cup water

1 cup (6$^{1}/_{2}$ ounces) granulated sugar

1 tablespoon light corn syrup

Pinch of kosher or fine-grained sea salt

$^{3}/_{4}$ cup (3$^{3}/_{4}$ ounces) finely chopped toasted, salted peanuts

PASTRY DOUGH: Briefly pulse together the flour, sugar, and salt in the work bowl of a food processor fitted with the steel blade. Cut the butter into small pieces and add. Pulse until the butter is cut into very tiny pieces, about 30 seconds. The texture will be sandy with very tiny lumps.

Use a fork to beat the egg yolk and vanilla together in a small bowl. With the food processor running, pour this mixture through the feed tube. Process until the dough wraps itself around the blade, about 1 minute. Shape the dough into a flat disk and tightly wrap in a double layer of plastic wrap. Chill in the refrigerator until firm before using, about 2 hours.

continued

Position a rack in the center of the oven and preheat to 375 degrees F. On a smooth, flat surface, roll out the pastry dough between sheets of lightly floured waxed or parchment paper to a large rectangle ¼ inch thick. Peel off the top piece of paper and brush off any excess flour. Use a 3-inch-round plain-edge cutter to cut out circles of dough. Place each circle in a tartlet pan and gently fit it to the bottom and sides of the pan, pushing it lightly into the fluted edges. Trim off any excess pastry dough at the top edge of the pan and patch any places that have holes or tears. Place the pans on a baking sheet, cover the top of each with another tartlet pan, and freeze for 15 minutes.

Bake the tartlet shells for 10 minutes then remove the top tartlet pans. Lightly pierce the bottom of the each tartlet shell with a fork to release air and prevent it from puffing up. Bake another 8–10 minutes, until light golden and set. Remove the baking sheet from the oven and transfer the tartlet pans to a rack to cool completely.

SALTED PEANUT CARAMEL FILLING: Heat the cream in a small saucepan over medium heat until it boils. At the same time in a 3-quart heavy-duty saucepan, combine the water, sugar, corn syrup, and salt and bring to a boil. Brush around the inside of the pan with a damp pastry brush at the point where the sugar syrup meets the sides of the pan. Do this twice during the cooking process to prevent the sugar from crystallizing. Cook over medium-high heat, without stirring, until the mixture turns amber, about 10 minutes.

Slowly pour the hot cream into the caramel mixture, stirring constantly. Be careful because the mixture will bubble and foam. Transfer the mixture to a medium bowl and let it cool for 10 minutes. Stir in the peanuts thoroughly. Use a 1½-inch ice cream scoop or a spoon to fill the tartlet shells with the filling. Let the tartlets set up at room temperature, about 30 minutes.

Gently slip the tartlets from the pans by carefully tapping the pans on the counter top. Serve the tartlets at room temperature.

KEEPING: The tartlets will keep tightly covered with aluminum foil, at room temperature, for up to 3 days.

STREAMLINING: The pastry dough can be made up to 4 days in advance and kept tightly wrapped in plastic wrap in the refrigerator. To freeze for up to 3 months, place in a freezer-safe bag. Label and date the package. If frozen, defrost overnight in the refrigerator and bring to room temperature before using.

The tartlet shells can be baked up to 2 days in advance and kept tightly wrapped in aluminum foil at room temperature.

Chocolate Dulce de Leche Pecan Pie

Makes 1 (10-inch) pie, 12 to 14 servings

This is one of those desserts that bowls over everyone. A light, flaky crust is filled with the perfect flavor combination of dulce de leche, bittersweet chocolate, and finely chopped pecans. The baked pie filling texture remains soft and slightly gooey which adds to taste sensation of this pie.

Special equipment: 1 (10-inch) deep pie dish

PIE DOUGH

8 tablespoons (4 ounces, 1 stick) unsalted butter

1¼ cups (5½ ounces) all-purpose flour

¼ teaspoon kosher or fine-grained sea salt

1 tablespoon granulated sugar

4 ounces cream cheese, chilled

2 to 3 tablespoons heavy whipping cream

CHOCOLATE DULCE DE LECHE FILLING

1 cup dark corn syrup

½ cup (3 ounces) firmly packed light brown sugar

2 large eggs, room temperature

1 tablespoon all-purpose flour

1 tablespoon (½ ounce) unsalted butter, melted

1 teaspoon pure vanilla extract

¼ teaspoon kosher or fine-grained sea salt

6 ounces bittersweet chocolate (66 to 72% cacao content), melted

¼ cup Dulce de Leche (page 34)

1¼ cups (5 ounces) pecans, finely chopped

GARNISH

32 pecan halves

PIE DOUGH: Cut the butter into small pieces and freeze for 20 minutes.

continued

Briefly pulse together the flour, salt, and sugar in the work bowl of a food processor fitted with a steel blade. Cut the cream cheese into small pieces and add to the dry ingredients in the food processor. Pulse until the cream cheese is cut into very tiny pieces. The texture should be sandy with very tiny lumps throughout. Then add the butter to the flour mixture and pulse until it is cut into pea size pieces, 30–45 seconds.

Remove the top of the food processor and sprinkle in 2 tablespoons of the cream. Replace the top and pulse for 10 seconds. Squeeze a small amount of the dough in your hand. If it holds together, don't add any more cream. If the dough is still very crumbly, add another tablespoon of cream, pulse to blend, then check the dough again. It won't hold together unless you squeeze it, but that's the texture you want.

Shape the dough into a flat disk and tightly wrap in a double layer of plastic wrap. Chill in the refrigerator until firm before using, at least 1 hour. If the dough is too firm it will splinter and break when rolled out. Let it stand at room temperature for 10–15 minutes to become more pliable.

On a smooth, flat surface, roll out the pie dough between sheets of lightly floured waxed or parchment paper to a large circle, about 12 inches. To tell if the dough will fit the pie pan, invert the pan over the dough. If there are 2–3 inches of dough that protrude beyond the sides of the pan, it will fit.

Carefully peel the paper off the top of the dough. Brush excess flour off of the dough then gently roll the pastry dough around the rolling pin. Place the pie pan directly underneath the rolling pin and carefully unroll the pastry dough into the pan. Or fold the dough in half. Carefully place it in half of the pie pan and gently unfold the dough. Carefully lift up the sides and fit the pie dough against the bottom and sides of the pie pan. Trim off the excess pie dough at the top of the pan and crimp or roll the edges.

Chill the pie pan in the freezer for 15–20 minutes. This helps prevent the pie dough from shrinking as it bakes and sets the butter in the dough, which helps to ensure flakiness.

Position a rack in the center of the oven and preheat to 350 degrees F.

CHOCOLATE DULCE DE LECHE FILLING: In a large bowl, whisk together the corn syrup, brown sugar, eggs, flour, butter, vanilla, and salt until thoroughly blended.

Add the chocolate, Dulce de Leche, and pecans and blend thoroughly. Transfer the filling to the pie pan. Arrange the pecan halves on top of the pie in concentric circles, leaving a little space between each. Place the pie pan on a baking sheet.

Bake the pie until the top is puffed and the center wiggles slightly, about 50 minutes. Remove the pie from the oven and transfer to a rack to cool completely. Serve slices of the pie at room temperature.

KEEPING: Store the pie loosely covered with waxed paper then tightly wrapped with aluminum foil, at room temperature, for up to 3 days.

STREAMLINING: The pie dough can be made in advance and kept in the refrigerator tightly wrapped in a double layer of plastic wrap for up to 4 days. To freeze for up to 3 months, wrap the dough tightly in several layers of plastic wrap and place it into a freezer bag. Label and date the package. If frozen, defrost overnight in the refrigerator before using. The pie dough can also be fit into the pie pan and frozen. Wrap as above and label.

TROUBLESHOOTING: Don't over process the pie dough or it will be tough and not flaky.

Cookies

Chocolate-Caramel Shortbread Bars

Makes 16 (4 x 1-inch) bars

These delicate, very full-flavored cookies bring together all my favorites. The dark brown sugar used to make the shortbread gives them a richer taste than traditional shortbread that is made with white sugar. But it is the dark chocolate and caramel mixture that is poured over the baked shortbread that takes these over the top. When you cut into the shortbread to make bars, cut cleanly all the way to the bottom of the pan so the bars separate squarely.

Special equipment: 1 (8-inch) square baking pan

SHORTBREAD

Nonstick baking spray

9 tablespoons (4^1/$_2$ ounces, 1 stick plus 1 tablespoon) unsalted butter, room temperature

^{1}/$_4$ cup (1^1/$_2$ ounces) firmly packed dark brown sugar

1^1/$_2$ cups (6^3/$_4$ ounces) all-purpose flour

^{1}/$_4$ teaspoon kosher or fine-grained sea salt

CHOCOLATE CARAMEL

10 ounces bittersweet (64 to 70% cacao content) chocolate, finely chopped

1^1/$_2$ cups (10 ounces) granulated sugar

^{1}/$_4$ cup water

6 tablespoons (3 ounces, ^{3}/$_4$ stick) unsalted butter, room temperature

1 cup heavy whipping cream

^{1}/$_2$ teaspoon kosher or fine-grained sea salt

Position a rack in the center of the oven and preheat to 350 degrees F. Line the baking pan with aluminum foil, letting it curl over the edges. Spray the foil with nonstick baking spray.

SHORTBREAD: Beat the butter in the bowl of an electric stand mixer using the flat beater attachment, or in a large bowl using a hand-held mixer, until fluffy, about 1 minute. Add the brown sugar and beat the mixture together until smooth and completely mixed.

continued

In a medium bowl, sift the flour. Add the salt and toss to blend. Add this mixture to the butter mixture, in 3 stages, blending completely.

Turn the dough out into the prepared pan. Dust your fingertips with flour and press the shortbread evenly into the pan.

Bake until golden brown, 25–30 minutes. Remove the pan from the oven and place on a cooling rack.

CHOCOLATE CARAMEL: Place the chocolate in a large bowl. Combine the sugar and water in a 3-quart heavy-duty saucepan. Cook over medium-high heat until the mixture begins to boil then brush around the inside of the pan with a damp pastry brush at the point where the sugar syrup meets the sides of the pan. Do this twice during the cooking process to prevent the sugar from crystallizing. Cook the mixture over high heat, without stirring, until it turns amber colored, 6–8 minutes.

When the mixture is amber colored, immediately add the butter, cream, and salt. Be very careful because the mixture will bubble and foam. Stir constantly with a heat-resistant spatula until the mixture is smooth, about 2 minutes.

Pour this mixture over the chocolate. Let stand for 1 minute then stir together until completely combined. Let the chocolate caramel stand for 8 minutes to cool, stirring frequently.

Pour the chocolate caramel over the shortbread in the pan. Cover the top of the pan tightly with plastic wrap. Refrigerate at least 4 hours or overnight, until the chocolate caramel is firm.

Use the edges of the aluminum foil to lift the shortbread from the pan then carefully peel the foil away from the shortbread. Use a large chef's knife dipped in warm water and dried to trim the edges of the shortbread. Cut the shortbread in half horizontally then cut each half into 8 equal bars, dipping the knife in warm water and drying between each cut. Serve the bars at room temperature.

KEEPING: Store the bars tightly covered with aluminum foil, at room temperature, for up to 3 days.

MAKING A CHANGE: Cut each 4-inch bar in half, making 2-inch bars.

Caramel Almond Shortbread Squares

Makes 24 (2-inch) squares

A classic shortbread crust is topped with a hefty layer of caramel and sliced raw almonds then baked together. The delicate shortbread and the caramel almond mixture make these squares both crunchy and chewy. And the lemon juice gives them a zesty flavor hint. For easier cutting, heat your knife blade in warm water then completely dry for each cut. Smaller, or larger, squares can be cut, if you wish.

Special equipment: 1 (9 x 13-inch) baking pan

SHORTBREAD CRUST

Nonstick baking spray

2 cups (9 ounces) all-purpose flour

1 cup (3 1/4 ounces) confectioners' sugar

16 tablespoons (8 ounces, 2 sticks) unsalted butter, chilled

CARAMEL ALMOND TOPPING

8 tablespoons (4 ounces, 1 stick) unsalted butter, melted

1 cup (6 ounces) firmly packed light brown sugar

2 tablespoons water

2 teaspoons freshly squeezed lemon juice

2 teaspoons pure vanilla extract

2 1/2 cups (7 3/4 ounces) sliced raw almonds

Position a rack in the center of the oven and preheat to 350 degrees F. Line the inside of the baking pan with aluminum foil that hangs over the short edges. Then spray the inside of the foil with nonstick baking spray.

SHORTBREAD CRUST: Briefly pulse together the flour and sugar in the work bowl of a food processor fitted with the steel blade. Cut the butter into small pieces and add. Pulse until the butter is cut into tiny pieces. Transfer the crust to the baking pan and pat it evenly across the bottom and into the corners.

Bake the crust for 15 minutes, until lightly colored. Remove from the oven and place the pan on a cooling rack while preparing the topping.

continued

CARAMEL ALMOND TOPPING: Combine the butter, brown sugar, water, lemon juice, and vanilla in a 3-quart heavy-duty saucepan over medium-high heat. Cook, stirring frequently, until the mixture comes to a boil. Remove the saucepan from the heat and immediately stir in the almonds, coating them completely with the caramel mixture.

Transfer the caramel almond mixture to the crust and spread it out evenly. Bake for 15 minutes, or until golden and set. Remove the baking pan from the oven, place on a rack, and cool completely.

To remove from the pan, lift with the edges of the aluminum foil then peel the foil gently away. Use a large chef's knife to cut into squares. Serve the squares at room temperature.

KEEPING: Store the squares between layers of waxed paper tightly wrapped in aluminum foil, at room temperature, for up to 3 days.

Pecan Butterscotch Cookies

Makes 60 (2-inch) round cookies

These light and crunchy cookies are the perfect snack. Butter and dark brown sugar are used to create a rich butterscotch flavor that is enhanced and heightened with the taste and texture of toasted pecans. If you do not have Demerara or turbinado sugar to roll your cookies in, you can use light or dark brown sugar or granulated white sugar.

Special equipment: 2 baking sheets

COOKIE DOUGH

$^2/_3$ cup (2$^1/_2$ ounces) shelled pecans

8 tablespoons (4 ounces, 1 stick) unsalted butter, softened

1 cup (6 ounces) firmly packed dark brown sugar

1 large egg, room temperature

1 large egg yolk, room temperature

$^1/_4$ teaspoon pure vanilla extract

1$^3/_4$ cups (7$^3/_4$ ounces) all-purpose flour

$^1/_4$ teaspoon baking soda

$^1/_2$ teaspoon cream of tartar

$^1/_4$ teaspoon kosher or fine-grained sea salt

TOPPING

1 large egg yolk, lightly beaten, room temperature

$^1/_2$ cup (3$^3/_4$ ounces) Demerara or turbinado sugar, divided

COOKIE DOUGH: Position a rack in the center of the oven and preheat to 350 degrees F. Place the pecans in a cake or pie pan and toast for 8 minutes. Remove the pan from the oven and transfer to a rack to cool. Using a chef's knife, finely chop the pecans on a cutting board.

Beat the butter in the bowl of an electric stand mixer using the flat beater attachment, or in a large bowl using a hand-held mixer, until fluffy, about 1 minute. Add the brown sugar and beat together until smooth and completely mixed.

Use a fork to lightly beat the egg, egg yolk, and vanilla together in a small bowl then add to the mixture. Beat together thoroughly.

continued

In a medium bowl, sift together the flour, baking soda, and cream of tartar. Add the salt and toss to blend. Add this mixture to the butter mixture, in 3 stages, stopping to scrape down the sides and bottom of the bowl after each addition. Add the pecans and blend thoroughly.

Divide the mixture in half and place each portion onto a large piece of waxed paper. Shape into rolls about 1 inch wide and 14 inches long. Tightly wrap each roll in the waxed paper and cover with plastic wrap. Chill the rolls in the refrigerator at least 12 hours.

Position the racks to the upper and lower thirds of the oven and preheat to 350 degrees F.

TOPPING: Unwrap the cookie rolls and brush the outside of each roll with egg yolk. Place ¼ cup sugar on each piece of waxed paper and roll each cookie roll in the sugar to completely coat the outside. Not all of the sugar will be used.

Line the baking sheets with parchment paper or nonstick liners. Cut each roll into ¼-inch-thick slices, turning the roll after 4 slices to keep it round. Place the slices on the baking sheets, leaving an inch of room between them. Sprinkle the remaining sugar on the tops of the cookies.

Bake for 5 minutes, switch the baking sheets on the oven racks, and bake another 5–6 minutes, until golden brown. Remove the baking sheets from the oven and cool completely on racks.

KEEPING: Store the cookies tightly covered with aluminum foil, at room temperature, for up to 3 days.

MAKING A CHANGE: Replace the toasted pecans with toasted walnuts.

STREAMLINING: The cookie rolls can be kept in the refrigerator for up to 4 days before baking. They can be frozen, tightly wrapped in layers of plastic wrap and aluminum foil and labeled, for up to 3 months.

ADDING STYLE: Make sandwich cookies using Dulce de Leche (page 34) for the filling.

Hazelnut Praline Biscotti

Makes about 42 biscotti

Praline is a mixture of nuts and caramelized sugar that is ground together after it cools. These twice-baked cookies use coarsely ground praline made with toasted hazelnuts. They are flavor packed with a crusty, yet slightly chewy texture. These cookies are great to dip into milk, hot chocolate, tea, or coffee, and biscotti travel very well so be sure to take a few on your next trip.

Special equipment: 1 baking sheet

2 cups (9 ounces) all-purpose flour

1^1/$_3$ cups (7 ounces) hazelnut Praline (page 36), coarsely chopped

^{1}/$_3$ cup (2 ounces) granulated sugar

^{1}/$_3$ cup (2 ounces) firmly packed light brown sugar

2 teaspoons baking powder

^{1}/$_4$ teaspoon kosher or fine-grained sea salt

2 extra-large eggs, room temperature

8 tablespoons (4 ounces, 1 stick) unsalted butter, melted

1 teaspoon pure vanilla extract

Position a rack in the center of the oven and preheat to 350 degrees F. Line the baking sheet with parchment paper or a nonstick liner.

Combine the flour, Praline, sugars, baking powder, and salt in the bowl of an electric stand mixer or a large bowl. Use the flat beater attachment or a hand-held mixer to blend together briefly on low speed.

Use a fork to lightly beat together the eggs, butter, and vanilla in a medium bowl. With the mixer speed on low, add this mixture to the dry ingredients and blend together thoroughly.

Divide the dough into 4 equal pieces. Dust your hands lightly with flour and shape each piece of dough into a loaf about 4–5 inches long, 2 inches wide, and ^{1}/$_2$ inch high. Place the loaves on the baking sheet, leaving several inches of space between them.

Bake the biscotti for 22–24 minutes, until the loaves are light golden and set. Remove the baking pan from the oven and cool on a rack for 10 minutes.

continued

Transfer the biscotti loaves to a cutting board. Using a serrated-edge knife, slice each loaf on the diagonal into $1/2$-inch-thick slices. Place these slices on their sides on the baking sheet. Bake for 15–20 minutes, until firm and golden colored.

Remove the pan from the oven and cool completely on a rack.

KEEPING: Store the biscotti in an airtight container between layers of waxed paper, at room temperature, for up to a week. To freeze for up to 3 months, wrap the container tightly in several layers of plastic wrap and aluminum foil. Label and date the package. If frozen, defrost overnight in the refrigerator and bring to room temperature before serving.

Dulce de Leche Sandwich Cookies

Makes 24 (1¹/₂-inch) sandwich cookies

If you haven't had dulce de leche (caramel made from sweetened condensed milk), you are in for a fabulous Latin American taste treat. The buttery cookies that are used to sandwich the Dulce de Leche offer a great flavor and texture combination. You can make both the Dulce de Leche and the cookies in advance then easily put together as many sandwiches as you would like right before you serve them.

Special equipment: 2 baking sheets and 1 (12-inch) pastry bag with a large round plain tip

COOKIES

6 ounces (12 tablespoons, 1¹/₂ sticks) unsalted butter, softened

¹/₂ cup (3 ounces) firmly packed dark brown sugar

2 teaspoons pure vanilla extract

2 cups (9 ounces) all-purpose flour

¹/₂ teaspoon kosher or fine-grained sea salt

DULCE DE LECHE FILLING

1 recipe Dulce de Leche (page 34)

COOKIES: Beat the butter in the bowl of an electric stand mixer using the flat beater attachment, or in a large bowl using a hand-held mixer, on medium speed until fluffy, about 1 minute. Add the brown sugar and beat together well. Stop occasionally and scrape down the sides and bottom of the bowl with a rubber spatula. Add the vanilla and blend thoroughly.

Sift the flour into a small bowl. Add the salt and toss to blend. Add this mixture to the butter mixture, in 3 stages, blending thoroughly after each addition.

Divide the dough in half and place each half on a large piece of waxed paper. Roll each piece of dough into a log about 1 inch wide and 8–10 inches long. Wrap the rolls tightly in the waxed paper and then in plastic wrap. Chill the logs 3–4 hours, or until firm.

Position the racks to the upper and lower thirds of the oven and preheat to 400 degrees F. Line the baking sheets with parchment paper or nonstick liners. Unwrap one cookie log and place it on a cutting board. Use a sharp knife and cut the log into ¹/₄-inch-thick slices. To keep the round shape of the log, roll it over slightly

continued

after a few slices. Place the slices on the baking sheets, leaving an inch of space between them. Repeat with the remaining cookie log.

Bake for 5 minutes. Switch the baking pans on the oven racks and bake another 5 minutes, until light golden. Remove the baking sheets from the oven and completely cool the cookies on the baking sheets on racks. Lift the cookies from the parchment paper and turn half of them so that their bottoms face up.

Fill the pastry bag partway with the Dulce de Leche. Pipe a small mound (about 1 inch) of Dulce de Leche in the center of the flat cookies then place another cookie on top of the filling, pressing down slightly to spread it to the edges.

KEEPING: Store the cookies, without the filling, tightly covered with aluminum foil, at room temperature, for up to 3 days. Store the filled cookies, at room temperature, for up to 2 days.

Caramel Crunch Shortbread Triangles

Makes 16 triangles

These buttery and flaky melt-in-your-mouth shortbread cookies are made in the traditional Scottish shortbread triangle shape. But unlike Scottish shortbread, they are made with dark brown sugar which gives them a richer flavor, and the chopped pecans add even more depth. The caramel garnish is cooked to the amber stage which dries quickly and firmly, giving the shortbread a slight crunchy texture. When the caramel drizzle is ready, you don't want to delay pouring it, so have the baked shortbread all cut and ready on the baking sheet. Also, it's best to use a saucepan that has a pour spout for cooking the caramel drizzle.

Special equipment: 1 (9^1/$_2$-inch) round, fluted-edge removable-bottom tart pan

SHORTBREAD TRIANGLES
Nonstick baking spray
^{2}/$_3$ cup pecans
8 tablespoons (4 ounces, 1 stick) unsalted butter, softened
^{1}/$_4$ cup (1^1/$_2$ ounces) firmly packed dark brown sugar
1 cup (4^1/$_2$ ounces) all-purpose flour
Pinch of kosher or fine-grained sea salt

CARAMEL CRUNCH DRIZZLE
^{1}/$_2$ cup (3^1/$_2$ ounces) granulated sugar
^{1}/$_4$ cup water
^{1}/$_8$ teaspoon cream of tartar

SHORTBREAD TRIANGLES: Spray the inside of the tart pan with nonstick baking spray. Position a rack in the center of the oven and preheat to 350 degrees F. Place the pecans in a cake or pie pan and toast for 8 minutes. Remove the pan from the oven and transfer to a rack to cool. Using a chef's knife, finely chop the pecans on a cutting board.

Beat the butter in the bowl of an electric stand mixer using the flat beater attachment, or in a large bowl using a hand-held mixer, until fluffy, about 1 minute. Add the brown sugar and beat the mixture together until smooth and thoroughly blended.

In a small bowl, sift the flour then add the salt and toss to blend. Add this mixture to the butter mixture, in 3 stages, stopping to scrape down the sides and bottom of the bowl after each addition. Add the pecans and blend thoroughly.

Transfer the mixture to the tart pan. Lightly dust your fingertips with flour and press the dough evenly into the tart pan. Score the shortbread into quarters then score each quarter into 4 equal triangles. Cover the tart pan tightly with plastic wrap and chill at least 1 hour before baking.

Position a rack in the center of the oven and preheat to 350 degrees F. Uncover the tart pan and place it on a baking sheet. Bake for 30–35 minutes until the shortbread is light golden colored. Remove the pan from the oven and transfer to a rack. Use a sharp knife to cut through the scored lines of the triangles then leave them to cool completely.

When the triangles are completely cool, gently remove the sides of the tart pan. Use a small offset spatula to transfer the triangles to a baking sheet or plate.

CARAMEL CRUNCH DRIZZLE: Place the sugar, water, and cream of tartar in a small saucepan and bring to a boil over high heat. Brush around the inside of the pan with a damp pastry brush at the point where the sugar syrup meets the sides of the pan. Do this twice during the cooking process to prevent the sugar from crystallizing. Cook the mixture over high heat, without stirring, until it turns amber colored, 6–8 minutes.

Drizzle the caramel over the shortbread triangles. It will set quickly. Let the shortbread stand for about 1 hour then use a small spatula to loosen them from the baking sheet or plate.

KEEPING: Store the shortbread tightly covered with aluminum foil, at room temperature, for up to 3 days.

MAKING A CHANGE: Replace the toasted pecans with toasted walnuts.

Nutty Caramel Bars

Makes 20 (2 1/4-inch) bars

These bars were inspired by my three very favorite nuts: pecans, walnuts, and almonds. An intense caramel mixture, using a large portion of these toasted and chopped nuts, makes up a thick topping that sits on a sweet light crust. These bars are very crunchy and chewy. Cut them with a serrated knife so that you can saw smoothly through the nuts and crust. They can be cut into smaller, or larger, sizes if you like. And you don't need any utensils to eat these, just serve with napkins.

Special equipment: 1 (9 x 13-inch) baking pan

CRUST

Nonstick baking spray
2 cups (9 ounces) all-purpose flour
2/3 cup (2 1/2 ounces) confectioners' sugar
Pinch of kosher or fine-grained sea salt
12 tablespoons (6 ounces, 1 1/2 sticks) unsalted butter, chilled

NUTTY CARAMEL TOPPING

1 1/2 cup (6 3/4 ounces) walnuts, coarsely chopped
1 cup (4 ounces) pecans, coarsely chopped
1 cup (5 ounces) whole unblanched almonds, coarsely chopped
1/2 cup (3 ounces) firmly packed light brown sugar
1/2 cup honey
11 tablespoons (5 1/2 ounces, 1 stick plus 3 tablespoons) unsalted butter, cut into small pieces
3 tablespoons heavy whipping cream

Position a rack in the center of the oven and preheat to 350 degrees F. Line the inside of the baking pan with aluminum foil that hangs over the short edges then spray the inside of the foil with nonstick baking spray.

CRUST: Briefly pulse together the flour, sugar, and salt in the work bowl of a food processor fitted with the steel blade. Cut the butter into small pieces and add. Pulse until the butter is cut into tiny pieces. Transfer the crust to the baking pan and pat it evenly across the bottom and into the corners.

Bake the crust for 20 minutes, until lightly colored. Remove from the oven and place on a cooling rack to cool completely.

continued

NUTTY CARAMEL TOPPING: Place the nuts on a rimmed baking sheet and toast in the oven for 10–12 minutes, until toasted and aromatic, stirring after 5 minutes. Remove the baking sheet from the oven and cool the nuts for 5 minutes.

Combine the brown sugar, honey, butter, and cream in a 3-quart heavy-duty saucepan over medium-high heat. Cook, stirring frequently, over medium-high heat until the mixture comes to a boil. Remove the saucepan from the heat and immediately stir in the nuts, coating them completely with the caramel mixture.

Transfer the nutty caramel mixture to the crust and spread it out evenly. Bake for 25 minutes, until golden and set. Remove the baking pan from the oven and cool completely on a rack.

Lift the mixture from the pan with the edges of the foil then peel the foil gently away. Use a large chef's knife to cut into 2¼-inch bars. Serve the bars at room temperature.

KEEPING: Store the bars between layers of waxed paper tightly wrapped in aluminum foil, at room temperature, for up to 3 days.

Cocoa and Caramel Sandwich Cookies

Makes about 40 (1¹/₂-inch) sandwich cookies

These tasty sandwich cookies are crunchy and gooey. The cookies, made with cocoa powder, add a bitter, yet mildly sweet flavor to the rich-cream honey-based caramel filling. Because the caramel from one cookie may slightly ooze out and stick to another cookie, be careful not to set them too close to each other. These are my husband's favorites with a cold glass of milk.

Special equipment: candy thermometer, 1 (8-inch) square baking pan, and 3 baking sheets

COCOA COOKIES

1¹/₂ cups (6³/₄ ounces) all-purpose flour

²/₃ cup (2¹/₂ ounces) cocoa powder, natural or Dutch processed

¹/₄ teaspoon kosher or fine-grained sea salt

1 cup (6¹/₂ ounces) granulated sugar

12 tablespoons (6 ounces, 1¹/₂ sticks) unsalted butter, chilled

1 large egg, room temperature

¹/₂ teaspoon pure vanilla extract

CARAMEL FILLING

Nonstick baking spray

2¹/₄ cups (14¹/₂ ounces) granulated sugar

1³/₄ cups heavy whipping cream

¹/₃ cup honey

1 tablespoon light corn syrup

4 tablespoons (2 ounces, ¹/₂ stick) unsalted butter, cut into small pieces

Pinch of kosher or fine-grained sea salt

1 tablespoon pure vanilla extract

COCOA COOKIES: Briefly pulse the flour, cocoa powder, salt, and sugar in the work bowl of a food processor fitted with the steel blade. Cut the butter into small pieces and add. Pulse until the butter is cut into tiny pieces.

continued

Use a fork to lightly beat together the egg and vanilla in a small bowl. With the food processor running, pour this mixture through the feed tube. Process until the dough wraps itself around the blade, about 1 minute. Shape the dough into a flat disk and cover tightly with plastic wrap. Chill until firm, about 3 hours.

CARAMEL FILLING: Line the baking pan with aluminum foil that fits snuggly and hangs a bit over the edges. Spray with nonstick baking spray.

Place the sugar, cream, honey, and corn syrup in a 3-quart heavy-duty saucepan over medium heat. Stir to dissolve the sugar. Increase the heat to medium high, place the candy thermometer in the pan, and cook, without stirring, until the mixture registers 250 degrees F. Turn off the heat and stir in the butter until it is completely melted then add the salt and vanilla and blend well. Turn the caramel into the prepared pan and place the pan on a wire rack to cool completely.

Position the racks to the upper and lower thirds of the oven and preheat to 400 degrees F. Line the baking sheets with parchment paper or nonstick liners. Roll out the cookie dough between sheets of lightly floured waxed or parchment paper to 1/4 inch thick. Use a 1 1/2-inch plain round cutter to cut out the cookies. Place them on the baking sheets, leaving about an inch of space between them. Gather the scraps back together, roll out, and cut out more cookies.

Bake for 6 minutes. Switch the baking sheets on the oven racks and bake another 6 minutes, until set. Remove the baking sheets from the oven and completely cool the cookies on the baking sheets on racks. Lift the cookies from the parchment paper and turn half of them with their bottoms facing up.

Lift the caramel from the pan using the edges of the foil. Use a 1-inch plain round cutter to cut out disks of the caramel. Place a caramel disk on the flat side of one cookie and top it with another cookie, pressing down lightly. If there are not enough caramel disks, gather some of the caramel together and press it into flat disks. Serve the cookies at room temperature.

KEEPING: Store the cookies without the filling tightly covered with aluminum foil, at room temperature, for up to 3 days. Store the filled cookies tightly covered with foil, at room temperature, for up to 2 days.

STREAMLINING: The cocoa cookie dough can be kept tightly covered in the refrigerator for up to 4 days before baking.

Custards, Mousses & Parfaits

Caramel Crème Brûlée

Makes 8 servings

This crème brûlée clearly and instantly delivers the full rich flavor of caramel. It has a slightly firm velvety consistency with an added sweet crispiness from the caramelized top. Make sure that you evenly distribute the granulated sugar on the surface of the cooled crème brûlée. I prefer to use a small propane kitchen torch to caramelize the top. Hold your canister at about a 45 degree angle 4–6 inches away from the top of the cooled crème brûlée. Then move it slowly back and forth until you see that all the sugar is caramelized.

Special equipment: 8 (³/4-cup) ramekins, custard cups, or bowls and 1 (3-quart) baking dish

CRÈME BRÛLÉE

1¼ cups (8 ounces) granulated sugar, divided

¼ cup water

1 teaspoon light corn syrup

1 cup half-and-half

2 cups heavy whipping cream

1½ teaspoons pure vanilla extract

6 large egg yolks, room temperature

½ teaspoon kosher or fine-grained sea salt

1 quart boiling water

GARNISH

¹/3 cup plus 1 tablespoon (2³/4 ounces) granulated sugar

Position a rack in the center of the oven and preheat to 325 degrees F. Place the ramekins in the baking dish.

CRÈME BRÛLÉE: Combine 1 cup and 2 tablespoons of the sugar, water, and corn syrup in a 3-quart heavy-duty saucepan. Cook over medium heat until the mixture comes to a boil, about 5 minutes. Brush around the inside of the pan with a damp pastry brush at the point where the sugar syrup meets the sides of the pan. Do this twice during the cooking process to prevent the sugar from crystallizing. Continue cooking until the mixture turns a deep amber color, 5–8 minutes.

At the same time, bring the half-and-half and cream to a boil in a small saucepan over medium heat. Add the vanilla then slowly add the hot cream mixture to the caramel mixture, stirring constantly with a heat-resistant

continued

spatula until the mixture is completely smooth. Remove the pan from the heat and transfer the mixture to a large bowl. Stir frequently to cool the mixture.

In a small bowl, whisk together the egg yolks, salt, and the remaining sugar. Whisk this mixture into the caramel cream mixture then strain to remove any lumps. Evenly divide the mixture among the ramekins, filling each ¾ full.

Carefully pour the water into the baking dish until it reaches halfway up the sides of the ramekins. Tightly cover the top of the dish with aluminum foil. Bake for 30–33 minutes, or until the custards look set on the edges but jiggle slightly in the center.

Remove the baking dish from the oven and remove the aluminum foil. Using a pair of tongs, remove the ramekins from the water bath and place them on a rack to cool completely. Cover the ramekins tightly with plastic wrap. Chill in the refrigerator for at least 2 hours.

GARNISH: To caramelize the tops, sprinkle the top of each custard evenly with 2 teaspoons of sugar. Use a propane kitchen torch to caramelize the sugar or place the ramekins on a baking sheet and place them under the broiler for 1–2 minutes. Cool slightly then serve.

KEEPING: Store the baked custard in the ramekins without the caramelized sugar on top, tightly covered with a double layer of plastic wrap, in the refrigerator for up to 3 days. Caramelize the tops right before serving.

Caramel Pots de Crème

Makes 6 servings

This custard dessert is very popular in France and Europe. The French *pot de crème* translates into pot of cream. The texture of this is very smooth and light; it virtually melts in your mouth. And although pot de crème can come in many flavors, I can easily say that caramel is my very favorite. I believe it will be yours, too. Be sure to prepare the pots de crème at least 3 hours in advance of serving so they have time to cool and chill.

Special equipment: 6 ($^1/_2$-cup) ramekins, custard cups, or bowls, 1 (3-quart) baking dish, and 1 (12-inch) pastry bag with a large open star tip

POTS DE CRÈME

1$^1/_4$ cups (8 ounces) granulated sugar
$^1/_4$ cup water
1$^1/_2$ cups heavy whipping cream
$^1/_2$ cup milk (whole, 2%, or 1%)
6 large egg yolks, room temperature
Pinch of kosher or fine-grained sea salt
1 teaspoon pure vanilla extract
1 quart boiling water

GARNISH

$^1/_4$ cup heavy whipping cream

POTS DE CRÈME: Position a rack in the center of the oven and preheat to 325 degrees F. Place the custard cups in the baking dish.

Combine the sugar and water in a 3-quart heavy-duty saucepan. Cook over medium heat until the mixture comes to a boil, about 5 minutes. Brush around the inside of the pan with a damp pastry brush at the point where the sugar syrup meets the sides of the pan. Do this twice during the cooking process to prevent the sugar from crystallizing. Continue cooking until the mixture turns a deep amber color, 5–8 minutes.

At the same time, bring the cream and milk to a boil in a small saucepan over medium heat. Slowly add the hot cream mixture to the caramel mixture, stirring constantly with a heat-resistant spatula until the mixture is completely smooth.

continued

In a large bowl, whisk together the egg yolks, salt, and vanilla. Add the caramel mixture slowly and whisk or stir together until thoroughly combined then strain the mixture into a large bowl.

Divide this mixture evenly into the ramekins. Carefully pour the water into the baking dish until it reaches halfway up the sides of the ramekins. Tightly cover the top of the pan with aluminum foil. Bake the custard for 25 minutes, or until it looks set on the edges but jiggles slightly in the center.

Remove the baking dish from the oven and remove the aluminum foil. Using a pair of tongs, remove the ramekins from the water bath and place them on a rack to cool completely. Cover the ramekins tightly with plastic wrap. Chill in the refrigerator for at least 2 hours before serving.

GARNISH: Whip the cream in the chilled bowl of an electric stand mixer using the wire whip attachment, or in a medium bowl using a hand-held mixer, until it holds firm peaks.

Fill the pastry bag partway with the whipped cream. Hold the pastry bag straight up and down about an inch above the top of the custard and pipe a star or rosette in the center. Serve the custards chilled.

KEEPING: Store the baked custard in the ramekins, tightly covered with a double layer of plastic wrap, in the refrigerator for up to 3 days.

Espresso Crème Caramel

Makes 6 servings

For coffee lovers this is the ultimate, intense caramel flavor with a shot of espresso. To assure the silkiness of the custard, make certain to stir constantly when mixing the hot milk into the egg mixture. The color of the custard and flow of the caramel make this dessert eye pleasing and mouthwatering.

Special equipment: 6 (^{1}/2-cup) ramekins, custard cups, or bowls and 1 (3-quart) baking dish

^{2}/3 cup (4 ounces) granulated sugar

^{1}/3 cup water

1^1/2 cups milk (whole or 2%)

^{1}/2 cup heavy whipping cream

^{1}/4 teaspoon kosher or fine-grained sea salt

2 teaspoons instant espresso powder

2 large eggs, room temperature

2 large egg yolks, room temperature

^{1}/2 teaspoon pure vanilla extract

^{1}/2 cup (3^1/2 ounces) granulated sugar

1 quart boiling water

Position a rack in the center of the oven and preheat to 350 degrees F. Place ramekins in the baking dish.

Combine the sugar and water in a small saucepan over medium-high heat. Bring the mixture to a boil. Cook, without stirring, until the mixture turns a rich golden brown, about 8 minutes. Divide the caramel evenly between the ramekins. Tilt and rotate each ramekin so the caramel completely covers the bottoms.

Warm the milk, cream, and salt in a 2-quart heavy-duty saucepan over medium heat until tiny bubbles form around the edges. Add the espresso powder and stir until it is completely dissolved, about 1 minute. Remove from the heat and cover the mixture to keep it warm for a few minutes.

Whip the eggs, egg yolks, and vanilla in the bowl of an electric stand mixer using the wire whip attachment, or in a large bowl using a hand-held mixer, until frothy. Slowly sprinkle on the sugar and whisk until well blended. In a steady stream, pour in the hot milk and mix thoroughly.

Strain the custard into a bowl or large liquid measuring cup. Pour the custard into the caramel-lined ramekins, dividing it evenly among them, and filling them almost to the top.

continued

PARIS

TOUR MAUGOURG 650

48 06 24 45

Place the baking dish on the oven rack. Carefully pour the water into the baking dish until it reaches halfway up the sides of the ramekins.

Bake for 30 minutes, until a toothpick or cake tester inserted in the center comes out clean. Remove the baking dish from the oven. Using a pair of tongs, remove the ramekins from the water bath and place them on a rack to cool completely. Cover the ramekins tightly with plastic wrap and chill in the refrigerator for several hours or overnight.

To unmold the custards, gently run a thin-blade knife around the sides of the ramekins. Place a serving plate over the top and invert the custard onto the plate. Repeat with each custard. Serve the custards cool.

KEEPING: Store the baked custard in the ramekins, tightly covered with a double layer of plastic wrap, in the refrigerator for up to 3 days.

MAKING A CHANGE: To intensify the espresso flavor, increase the instant espresso powder to 1 tablespoon.

Classic Butterscotch Pudding

Makes 8 servings

Dark brown sugar and butter give this pudding its pronounced 'to-die-for' butterscotch flavor. The whipped cream garnish offers just a slight amount of delightful flavor contrast. The texture is smooth, silky, and dense. To add a little extra flair, use sturdy clear glass bowls or glasses to serve the pudding.

Special equipment: 8 (1-cup) ramekins, bowls, or glasses and
1 (12-inch) pastry bag with a large open star tip

PUDDING

1 $3/4$ cups milk (whole, 2%, or 1%)

1 $1/2$ cups heavy whipping cream

6 tablespoons (3 ounces, $3/4$ stick) unsalted butter, cut into small pieces

1 $1/4$ cups (7 $1/2$ ounces) firmly packed dark brown sugar

3 large egg yolks, room temperature

$1/4$ cup cornstarch, sifted

$1/4$ teaspoon kosher or fine-grained sea salt

2 teaspoons pure vanilla extract

GARNISH

$1/4$ cup heavy whipping cream

PUDDING: In a 3-quart heavy-duty saucepan, bring the milk and cream to a boil over medium heat. Turn off the heat and set aside for a few minutes.

In a large heavy-duty saucepan, melt the butter over medium heat. Add the brown sugar and raise the heat. Cook, stirring constantly, with a heat-resistant spatula for 5 minutes to caramelize the mixture.

Stirring constantly, add the brown sugar mixture to the hot milk mixture. Whisk until smooth, about 30 seconds.

Place the egg yolks in a medium bowl. Add $3/4$ cup of the hot mixture and whisk constantly to temper the egg yolks. Add the cornstarch and salt and whisk until smooth. Add this mixture to the milk mixture in the saucepan and cook, stirring constantly, over medium-high heat until thick. The mixture will begin to bubble when it is ready. Turn off the heat and stir in the vanilla.

continued

Divide the pudding evenly between the ramekins. Cover tightly with plastic wrap and chill thoroughly, at least 2 hours, before serving.

GARNISH: Whip the cream in the bowl of an electric stand mixer using the wire whip attachment, or in a large bowl using a hand-held mixer, until it holds soft peaks. Fill the pastry bag partway with the whipped cream. Pipe a rosette of whipped cream in the center of each pudding no longer than 2 hours before serving.

KEEPING: The pudding will keep, tightly covered, in the refrigerator for up to 3 days.

Mini Caramel Soufflés

Makes 8 mini soufflés

Like all soufflés, this is light, fluffy, and airy. But what makes this one unusual is its rich caramel flavor. The trick is to use Classic Caramel Sauce in the mixture and as a garnish. Always serve these immediately after baking while the tops are nicely puffed and they are warm.

Special equipment: 8 (¼-cup) soufflé dishes, ramekins, or bowls

SOUFFLÉS

1 tablespoon (½ ounce) unsalted butter, melted
3 tablespoons granulated sugar, divided
½ recipe Classic Caramel Sauce (page 33)
1 large egg yolk, room temperature
3 large egg whites, room temperature
Pinch of cream of tartar

GARNISH

Confectioners' sugar
Classic Caramel Sauce (page 33)

Position a rack in the center of the oven and preheat to 425 degrees F. Use a pastry brush to coat the inside of the soufflé dishes with butter. Then completely dust the insides using 1 tablespoon sugar, tilting them as needed.

In a medium bowl, whisk together the caramel sauce and the egg yolk. Whip the egg whites in the bowl of an electric stand mixer using the wire whip attachment, or in a large bowl using a hand-held mixer, until frothy. Add the cream of tartar and continue to whip, slowly adding the remaining sugar, until the whites hold soft peaks.

Fold ¼ of the whipped egg whites into the caramel sauce mixture. Then fold in the remaining egg whites, in 3 stages, being careful not to deflate the mixture. Use a 2-inch ice cream scoop to divide the mixture evenly among the soufflé dishes and place them on a baking sheet. Bake for 14 minutes, or until puffed and golden brown.

GARNISH: Remove the baking sheet from the oven, lightly dust the tops of the soufflés with the sugar, and serve immediately with Classic Caramel Sauce for garnish.

ADDING STYLE: Serve sliced fresh peaches or fresh raspberries on the side.

Caramel Mousse

Makes 4 to 6 servings

This irresistible mousse is very light and airy, with intense caramel flavor. And the hints of honey and vanilla add even more depth to this instantly enjoyable dessert. For more generous portion sizes, serve this mousse from a large bowl instead of using individual serving bowls.

Special equipment: 1 (12-inch) pastry bag with a large open star tip

2 cups heavy whipping cream, divided
1/2 cup (3 1/2 ounces) granulated sugar
1/2 cup (3 ounces) firmly packed light brown sugar
1/4 cup water
2 teaspoons honey
1 teaspoon pure vanilla extract
4 tablespoons (2 ounces, 1/2 stick) unsalted butter, softened

Bring 2/3 cup of the cream to a boil in a small saucepan over medium heat. Cook the sugars, water, honey, and vanilla in a 2-quart heavy-duty saucepan over high heat until the mixture comes to a boil. Brush around the inside of the pan with a damp pastry brush at the point where the sugar syrup meets the sides of the pan. Do this twice during the cooking process to prevent the sugar from crystallizing. Cook the mixture over high heat, without stirring, until it turns amber colored, 6–8 minutes.

Lower the heat to medium and slowly add the hot cream to the sugar mixture while stirring constantly. The cream will bubble and foam. Continue to stir to make sure there are no lumps. Remove the saucepan from the heat and stir in the butter until it is completely melted.

Transfer the caramel mixture to a large bowl, cover tightly with plastic wrap, cool to room temperature, then chill until thick, about 2 hours.

Whip the remaining cream in the bowl of an electric stand mixer using the wire whip attachment, or in a large bowl using a hand-held mixer, until it holds soft peaks. Fold the whipped cream into the chilled caramel mixture, in 3 stages.

Fill the pastry bag partway with the mousse. Pipe the mousse into serving bowls or martini glasses. Serve at room temperature.

KEEPING: The mousse will keep, tightly covered with plastic wrap, in the refrigerator for up to 2 days.

Caramel Milk Chocolate Mousse

Makes 6 servings

Caramel and milk chocolate come together to make a mousse with a perfect balance of flavor and texture. Because the mousse needs time to set, make it at least 4 hours before serving.

Special equipment: 6 (¹/₂-cup) ramekins, custard cups, or bowls, and
  1 (12-inch) pastry bag with a large open star tip

4 ounces dark milk chocolate (38 to 42% cacao content), finely chopped
¹/₃ cup (3¹/₂ ounces) granulated sugar
¹/₄ cup water
3 tablespoons (1¹/₂ ounces) unsalted butter, softened
1³/₄ cups heavy whipping cream, divided

Melt the chocolate in the top of a double boiler over low heat, stirring often, or in a microwave-safe bowl on lowest power for 30 second bursts, stirring in between each burst. Remove the top pan of the double boiler and wipe dry or remove the bowl from the microwave.

Cook the sugar and water in a 2-quart heavy-duty saucepan over high heat until the mixture comes to a boil. Brush around the inside of the pan with a damp pastry brush at the point where the sugar syrup meets the sides of the pan. Do this twice during the cooking process to prevent the sugar from crystallizing. Cook the mixture over high heat, without stirring, until it turns amber colored, 6–8 minutes. Lower the heat to medium and stir in the butter until it is completely melted.

Slowly add ¹/₂ cup of the cream to the caramel mixture while stirring constantly. The cream will bubble and foam. Remove the saucepan from the heat and let the mixture cool slightly.

Whip the remaining cream in the bowl of an electric stand mixer using the wire whip attachment, or in a large bowl using a hand-held mixer, until it holds soft peaks. Set aside ⅓ cup of the whipped cream for garnish.

Whisk together the melted chocolate and caramel until smooth. If the mixture is warm, let it cool to room temperature. Fold the whipped cream into the caramel milk chocolate mixture, in 3 stages.

Use a 2-inch ice cream scoop or a large spoon to transfer the mousse into the ramekins. Cover tightly with plastic wrap and chill for at least 4 hours to set up.

For the garnish, fill the pastry bag partway with the reserved whipped cream. Pipe a rosette or star in the center of each mousse no longer than 3 hours before serving.

KEEPING: The mousse will keep, tightly covered with plastic wrap, in the refrigerator for up to 2 days.

Tropical Mascarpone Parfait

Makes 4 servings

Pineapple and mixed nuts give this parfait a tropical taste that is further boosted with a flavor-charged mixture of mascarpone and Classic Caramel Sauce. The sweet cream and very subtle tanginess of the mascarpone offer a refreshing spike to this dessert. Before caramelizing the pineapple chunks, be sure to drain off any liquid and pat them as dry as possible with paper towels. For backyard and picnic gatherings, try making your parfaits in disposal 8-ounce cups.

Special equipment: 4 wine or parfait glasses

8 tablespoons (4 ounces, 1 stick) unsalted butter, cut into small pieces
4 cups pineapple chunks (fresh or canned)
4 tablespoons firmly packed light brown sugar
Pinch of kosher or fine-grained sea salt
16 ounces mascarpone
2 recipes Classic Caramel Sauce (page 33), chilled

GARNISH
¹/₂ cup (2¹/₂ ounces) coarsely chopped toasted mixed nuts

Melt the butter over medium heat in a large skillet or saucepan. Add the pineapple and sprinkle with the brown sugar and salt. Stir the mixture and sauté the pineapple until it is caramelized, about 5 minutes. Transfer the pineapple to a large bowl and let it cool to room temperature.

Place the mascarpone and caramel sauce in the bowl of an electric stand mixer or a large bowl. Use the flat beater attachment or a hand-held mixer to beat the mixture together until it is smooth and completely blended, about 2 minutes.

To assemble the parfaits, spoon about 1¹/₂ inches of the pineapple chunks into the bottom of each glass. Spoon a layer of the caramel-mascarpone mixture onto the pineapple then repeat with another layer of pineapple and caramel mascarpone, filling the glass almost to the top.

GARNISH: Sprinkle 2 tablespoons of the nuts on top of each parfait. Serve at room temperature or chilled.

KEEPING: Cover the glasses tightly with plastic wrap and refrigerate for up to 3 hours before serving.

MAKING A CHANGE: Replace the pineapple chunks with bananas.

Caramelized Apple Parfait

Makes 4 servings

This yogurt-based parfait is refreshing, nutritious, very easy to make, and most importantly, it is scrumptious. Caramelized fresh apples are layered between tangy non-fat plain Greek yogurt. The contrast between the sweetness of the caramelized apples and slightly tart yogurt offers a very enjoyable taste experience. This parfait is topped off with a sprinkle of spicy ground cinnamon. Use your favor apples to make this.

Special equipment: 4 wine or parfait glasses

6 medium apples, such as Granny Smith or Gala

4 tablespoons (2 ounces, $^1/_2$ stick) unsalted butter, cut into small pieces

3 tablespoons firmly packed light brown sugar, divided

$^1/_4$ teaspoon ground cinnamon

$^1/_4$ teaspoon freshly grated lemon zest

Pinch of kosher or fine-grained sea salt

$^1/_2$ teaspoon pure vanilla extract

3 cups plain non-fat Greek yogurt

GARNISH

1 teaspoon ground cinnamon

Peel the apples, cut them into quarters, and remove the core from each quarter. Cut each quarter in half lengthwise and cut these into $^1/_2$-inch pieces. Place the apple pieces in a large bowl.

Melt the butter over medium heat in a large skillet or saucepan. Add the apples and sprinkle with $1^1/_2$ tablespoons of the brown sugar. Stir the mixture and sauté the apples until they are tender, about 7–8 minutes.

Sprinkle the remaining brown sugar, cinnamon, lemon zest, salt, and vanilla onto the apples. Stir the mixture and cook another 3–4 minutes, until the apples are caramelized. Transfer the apples to a large bowl and let them cool to room temperature.

continued

To assemble the parfaits, whisk the yogurt until it is completely smooth. Spoon about $1^{1}/_{2}$ inches of the apple mixture into the bottom of each glass. Spoon a layer of yogurt onto the apples then repeat with another layer of apples and yogurt, filling the glass.

GARNISH: Lightly sprinkle cinnamon on top of each parfait. Serve at room temperature or chilled.

KEEPING: Cover the glasses tightly with plastic wrap and refrigerate for up to 3 hours before serving.

MAKING A CHANGE: Sprinkle freshly grated nutmeg on top of the parfaits instead of cinnamon.

Caramel
Candies

Classic Cream Caramels

Makes 64 (1-inch) caramels

This caramel candy is as close to pure caramel flavor as you can get. It's slightly firm with a smooth texture. To serve them, I like to wrap each piece individually in clear waxed paper and place them in a shallow bowl. To get the full caramel experience, I suggest placing a piece in your mouth and letting it melt some before chewing.

Special equipment: candy thermometer and 1 (8-inch) square baking pan

Nonstick baking spray
$1\frac{1}{2}$ cups (10 ounces) granulated sugar
$\frac{3}{4}$ cup light corn syrup
$1\frac{1}{2}$ tablespoons ($\frac{3}{4}$ ounce) unsalted butter, softened
$1\frac{1}{2}$ cups heavy whipping cream
$\frac{1}{8}$ teaspoon kosher or fine-grained sea salt
$1\frac{1}{2}$ teaspoons pure vanilla extract
1 tablespoon canola or safflower oil

Line the baking pan with aluminum foil, letting it extend over the edges. Spray the foil with nonstick baking spray.

In a 3-quart heavy-duty saucepan, combine the sugar and corn syrup. Cook over medium heat, stirring constantly with a heat-resistant spatula, until the mixture comes to a boil, about 5 minutes. Brush around the inside of the pan with a damp pastry brush at the point where the sugar syrup meets the sides of the pan. Do this twice during the cooking process to prevent the sugar from crystallizing.

Place the candy thermometer in the pan, increase the heat to medium high, and cook the mixture, without stirring, until it registers 305 degrees F, about 15 minutes. Stir in the butter, keeping the mixture boiling. When checking the temperature with your candy thermometer, make sure you hold it straight up and down and that the bottom of the thermometer is in the mixture, not sitting on the bottom of the pan.

In a 1-quart saucepan, bring the cream to a boil. Slowly add the cream to the caramel mixture, stirring constantly, until the mixture registers 250 degrees F on the candy thermometer, about 10 minutes.

continued

Classic
CARAMEL

Remove the pan from the heat and let it stand for 5 minutes then stir in the salt and vanilla. Pour the caramel into the prepared pan, cover tightly with plastic wrap, and let stand at room temperature for at least 8 hours to set up.

Coat a cutting board and the blade of a large chef's knife with the oil. Lift the caramel from the pan by holding the aluminum foil. Carefully peel the foil away from the caramel and place it on the cutting board. Cut the caramel into 8 (1-inch) strips then cut each strip into 8 pieces. Serve the candies at room temperature.

KEEPING: Store the caramels between layers of waxed paper in a tightly covered container, at room temperature, for up to 2 weeks.

MAKING A CHANGE: Add 1 cup roughly chopped, toasted nuts to the mixture when adding the salt and vanilla.

To make Fleur de Sel caramels, eliminate the salt and add 1 teaspoon Fleur de Sel to the caramel mixture. Evenly sprinkle the top of the caramels with a teaspoon of Fleur de Sel before they set up.

ADDING STYLE: Dip the caramels into bittersweet chocolate or drizzle lines of bittersweet chocolate over the top of the caramels.

For Fleur de Sel caramels, sprinkle the top of each caramel with a few grains of Fleur de Sel after dipping in chocolate.

Chocolate-Dipped Espresso Caramels

Makes 64 (1-inch) squares

Coffee and dark chocolate lovers are in for a treat with this candy. Espresso is infused into a caramel candy mixture creating a zingy taste sensation that releases its full flavor as it is chewed. The dark chocolate coating, along with the few pieces of cashew nuts, offers more flavor depth and a bit of crunchiness. Make sure to sprinkle the nuts on right after you dip the caramels; that way they will set up in the chocolate. I like to serve these with after dinner drinks like dessert wines and fortified liquors.

Special equipment: candy thermometer and 1 (8-inch) square baking pan

CARAMELS
2 tablespoons canola or safflower oil, divided

1^1/$_2$ cups heavy whipping cream

2 cups (13 ounces) granulated sugar

^{1}/$_3$ cup honey

^{1}/$_2$ cup light corn syrup

2 tablespoons (1 ounce) unsalted butter, softened

1 tablespoon instant espresso powder dissolved in 1 tablespoon water

GARNISH
12 ounces semisweet or bittersweet chocolate (56 to 72% cacao content)

^{1}/$_4$ cup (1^1/$_4$ ounces) coarsely chopped toasted cashews

Line baking pan with aluminum foil, letting it extend over the sides. Use a paper towel to coat the bottom and sides of the foil with 1 tablespoon of the oil.

In a 3-quart heavy-duty saucepan, bring the cream to a boil over medium heat. Add the sugar, honey, and corn syrup. Stir to blend then bring the mixture back to a boil. Brush around the inside of the pan with a damp pastry brush at the point where the sugar syrup meets the sides of the pan. Do this twice during the cooking process to prevent the sugar from crystallizing.

continued

Increase the heat to medium-high, place a candy thermometer in the pan, and cook the mixture, stirring occasionally with a heat-resistant spatula, until it registers 257 degrees F on the thermometer, about 12 minutes.

Remove the pan from the heat and stir in the butter until it is completely melted. Then stir in the liquid espresso. Pour the mixture into the prepared pan and place the pan on a cooling rack. Let the caramel cool completely, at room temperature, 2–3 hours.

With the remaining oil, coat a cutting board and the blade of a large chef's knife. Lift the candy from the pan by holding the edges of the aluminum foil. Invert the caramel onto the cutting board and peel off the foil. Cut the caramel evenly into 1-inch squares.

Very finely chop the chocolate. Melt ¾ of it in the top of a double boiler over hot water, stirring often, or in a microwave-safe bowl for 30 second bursts, stirring after each burst. Remove the top pan of the double boiler and wipe it completely dry or remove the bowl from the microwave. In 3 stages, stir in the remaining chocolate, making sure each batch is melted before adding the next.

Line a baking sheet with waxed or parchment paper. Place the pan of chocolate over a pan of warm water, making sure it fits tightly. Dip a caramel in the chocolate then use a plastic fork with the middle tines broken out to remove the caramel from the chocolate, letting any excess drip off. Place the dipped caramel onto the baking sheet. After dipping 6 caramels, sprinkle the tops with the cashews. Repeat with the remaining caramels. Let the chocolate set at room temperature or place the baking sheet in the refrigerator for 15 minutes. Peel the caramels off of the paper and serve at room temperature.

KEEPING: Store the caramels between sheets of waxed paper in a tightly covered container, at room temperature, for up to 2 weeks.

Caramel Chocolate Truffles

Makes 24 (1-inch) round truffles

These chewy dark chocolate morsels offer a perfect flavor balance of caramel and dark chocolate. If you serve these a day or two after making them, you may want to re-roll them in cocoa powder right before serving. These are great as an after dessert treat with coffee or tea.

Special equipment: 1 baking sheet

1 cup (6^1/$_2$ ounces) granulated sugar
^{1}/$_4$ cup water
1 teaspoon light corn syrup
^{1}/$_2$ cup heavy whipping cream
1 teaspoon pure vanilla extract
5 ounces bittersweet chocolate (66 to 72% cacao), finely chopped
^{1}/$_2$ cup (2 ounces) cocoa powder, natural or Dutch processed

Combine the sugar, water, and corn syrup in a 2-quart heavy-duty saucepan and place over medium-high heat. When the mixture begins to boil, brush around the inside of the pan with a damp pastry brush at the point where the sugar syrup meets the sides of the pan. Do this twice during the cooking process to prevent the sugar from crystallizing. Cook over high heat without stirring until it is a dark amber color, about 9 minutes.

While the sugar mixture is cooking, bring the cream to a boil in a ^{1}/$_2$-quart saucepan. When the sugar mixture has reached the dark amber stage, add the cream and stir with a heat-resistant spatula until the mixture is smooth. Be careful because the cream will bubble and foam. Remove the pan from the heat and stir in the vanilla.

Transfer the mixture to a large glass bowl and add the chocolate. Stir until it is completely melted. Cover the bowl with plastic wrap, cool completely, and let stand at room temperature until it is thick, 6–8 hours. Or refrigerate for about 1 hour to thicken.

Line a baking sheet with waxed or parchment paper. Use a 1-inch ice cream scoop to scoop out balls of the truffle mixture, placing them on the baking sheet. Sift the cocoa powder into a small bowl. Dust your hands lightly with cocoa powder and roll the truffles into balls then roll them in the cocoa powder to coat them completely. Serve the truffles, at room temperature, in pleated paper candy cups.

KEEPING: Store the truffles between layers of waxed paper in a tightly covered container in the refrigerator for up to 1 week. Bring the truffles to room temperature before serving.

MAKING A CHANGE: Use 7 ounces of dark milk chocolate in place of the bittersweet chocolate.

Chocolate Caramel Pecan Clusters

Makes 60 clusters

It's hard to do better than the flavor combination of pecans, caramel, and chocolate. Roasted pecan halves make up the foundation of these candies. They are covered with a generous amount of rich caramel mixture that is then topped with melted bittersweet chocolate. These candies are chewy with just a little crunchiness from the pecans. Try making interesting designs with your pecan halves for each of your clusters.

Special equipment: candy thermometer and 2 baking sheets

5 cups (1 pound plus 4 ounces) pecan halves
1 cup heavy whipping cream
1/2 cup light corn syrup
1/2 cup (3 ounces) firmly packed light brown sugar
1/3 cup (2 ounces) granulated sugar
2 tablespoons (1 ounce) unsalted butter, softened
2 teaspoons pure vanilla extract
1 pound bittersweet (64 to 72% cacao content) chocolate, finely chopped

Line 2 baking sheets with aluminum foil or nonstick liners. If you use foil, wipe a thin layer of vegetable oil with a paper towel on the surface to prevent unnecessary sticking. On each baking sheet, arrange 30 clusters of 4 pecan halves each, leaving an inch of space between them.

In a 2-quart heavy-duty saucepan, combine the cream, corn syrup, sugars, and butter. Cook over medium heat, stirring frequently with a heat-resistant spatula, until the mixture comes to a boil, about 7 minutes. Brush around the inside of the pan with a damp pastry brush at the point where the sugar syrup meets the sides of the pan. Do this twice during the cooking process to prevent the sugar from crystallizing.

Increase the heat to medium-high, place the candy thermometer in the pan, and cook the mixture, stirring constantly, until it registers 246 degrees F on the thermometer, about 15 minutes. Remove the pan from the heat and stir in the vanilla. Transfer the caramel to a large bowl and stir to cool slightly, about 2 minutes.

Spoon a tablespoon of caramel onto the center of each pecan cluster. Let the caramel completely set, at room temperature, for about 30 minutes.

Melt ¾ of the chocolate in the top of a double boiler over low heat, stirring often, or in a microwave-safe bowl on lowest power for 30 second bursts, stirring in between each burst. Remove the top pan of the double boiler and wipe dry or remove the bowl from the microwave. In 3 stages, stir in the remaining chocolate, making sure each batch is melted before adding the next.

Spoon a tablespoon of chocolate over the caramel on each cluster. Let the chocolate set at room temperature, about 45 minutes, or chill in the refrigerator for 15 minutes. Peel the clusters off of the aluminum foil. Serve them at room temperature. Don't stack or allow the clusters to touch each other because they may stick together.

KEEPING: Store the clusters between layers of waxed paper in an airtight container in the refrigerator, for up to 1 month.

MAKING A CHANGE: Replace the pecans with whole unblanched almonds or walnut halves. Replace the bittersweet chocolate with dark milk or white chocolate.

PIPPIN LAKE LOOKING NORTH
MOUND LOCATED ON THE
GEO. B. TOWNE FARM

Caramel-Filled Marzipan Coins

Makes 12 coins

If you're not a marzipan lover these will convert you. The almond flavor of the marzipan is a perfect marriage with the slightly nutty and toasty Classic Caramel Sauce. A bittersweet chocolate topping adds even more depth to these yummy candies. If the marzipan becomes sticky, sprinkle a small amount of confectioners' sugar on the parchment or waxed paper. Because marzipan is so malleable, use a small metal spatula to transfer the coins onto a serving plate. Try these as an after dinner sweet treat with tea, coffee, or liquors.

Special equipment: 1 baking sheet

1 roll (7 ounces) marzipan
3 tablespoons Classic Caramel Sauce (page 33)
2 ounces semisweet or bittersweet chocolate (56 to 72% cacao content), finely chopped

Line the baking sheet with parchment or waxed paper. Slice the roll of marzipan into 12 (¾-inch-thick) pieces and place on the baking sheet.

Use the back of a ½ teaspoon measuring spoon to press gently into the center of each piece of marzipan, making an indentation. Spoon about ½ teaspoon of the caramel sauce into each indentation.

Melt the chocolate in the top of a double boiler or in a microwave oven on low power for 30-second bursts. Stir the chocolate often in the double boiler or after each microwave burst.

When the chocolate is completely melted, transfer it to a small parchment paper pastry bag or a plastic bag that closes securely on top. If using the pastry bag, fold the top down securely and snip off a tiny opening at the pointed end. If using a plastic bag, secure the top, squeeze the chocolate toward one pointed end of the bag, and snip off a tiny opening.

Hold the bag over the center of one of the marzipan coins and squeeze chocolate onto the caramel sauce, covering most of it. Repeat with the remaining marzipan coins. Place the baking sheet in the refrigerator to set the chocolate for 15 minutes. Serve the marzipan coins at room temperature.

KEEPING: The marzipan coins will keep at room temperature, tightly covered with aluminum foil, for up to 3 days.

MAKING A CHANGE: Replace the dark chocolate with dark milk chocolate.

Golden Mixed Nut Brittle

Makes about 40 irregular-shaped pieces

This intensely sweet golden-color brittle is mellowed out by the warm buttery flavor of mixed nuts. Although this brittle has a crunchy bite, the nuts make it chewy. It's easy to break the finished brittle into varying sizes.

Special equipment: 1 jelly roll pan

2 cups (14 ounces) granulated sugar
1/2 cup water
1/2 teaspoon cream of tartar
2 cups (9 ounces) toasted, salted mixed nuts

Line the jelly roll pan with a nonstick silicone mat.

Combine the sugar, water, and cream of tartar in a 3-quart heavy-duty saucepan over medium-high heat. When the mixture begins to boil, brush around the inside of the pan with a damp pastry brush at the point where the sugar syrup meets the sides of the pan. Do this twice during the cooking process to prevent the sugar from crystallizing. Cook over high heat, without stirring, until it is a medium caramel color, about 9 minutes.

Add the nuts and stir with a heat-resistant spatula to coat them completely with the caramel. Remove the pan from the heat, pour the mixture onto the silicone mat on the jelly roll pan, and spread it out with the spatula. Work quickly because the mixture sets up rapidly.

Let the nut brittle cool completely, about 30 minutes, then break it into pieces with your hands.

KEEPING: Store the brittle between layers of waxed paper in a tightly covered container, at room temperature, for up to 1 week.

MAKING A CHANGE: Use a single type of toasted nut instead of the mixed nuts.

Bittersweet Chocolate Salted Toffee

Makes about 60 pieces

This is toffee taken to the next level with the addition of toasted almonds and dark chocolate. The Fleur de Sel sea salt helps bring forward all the flavors. And unlike traditional toffee that can be firm, this toffee is crunchy and chewy. Break the toffee into small-bite sizes. Adjust the amount of Fleur de Sel that you sprinkle on top to your desired taste.

Special equipment: candy thermometer and 1 (2-quart) baking pan

1 cup (3 ounces) sliced almonds

1 tablespoon canola or safflower oil

16 tablespoons (8 ounces, 2 sticks) unsalted butter, cut into small pieces

3/4 cup (4 1/2 ounces) firmly packed light brown sugar

3 tablespoons water

1/4 teaspoon kosher or fine-grained sea salt

1/4 teaspoon baking soda

1 teaspoon pure vanilla extract

12 ounces bittersweet chocolate (64 to 72% cacao content), finely chopped

2 tablespoons coarse sea salt, such as Fleur de Sel

Position a rack in the center of the oven and preheat to 350 degrees F. Place the almonds in a cake or pie pan and toast in the oven for 12–14 minutes, until light golden. Shake the pan every 5 minutes to stir the almonds. Remove the pan from the oven and cool completely then finely chop the almonds.

Line the baking pan with aluminum foil that fits snuggly and hangs a bit over the edges. Use a paper towel to oil the inside of the foil.

Melt the butter in a 3-quart heavy-duty saucepan over medium heat. Add the sugar, water, and salt and cook, stirring constantly, until the mixture registers 260 degrees F on a candy thermometer.

Immediately stir in the almonds and continue cooking the mixture until it becomes golden brown and registers 290 degrees F on the thermometer. Immediately stir in the baking soda and vanilla. Be very careful as the mixture will bubble and foam.

continued

Turn the toffee out into the prepared pan and spread it into the edges. Quickly sprinkle the top of the toffee evenly with the chocolate. Let it stand for 2 minutes and it will begin to melt. Use a small offset spatula to spread the chocolate evenly over the top of the toffee.

Let the chocolate begin to set up at room temperature, about 15 minutes, then sprinkle the top of the chocolate evenly with a little of the sea salt. If the salt disappears into the chocolate, wait another 5–10 minutes then sprinkle the salt over the top. Let the toffee set up at room temperature until firm, about 30 minutes, then chill in the refrigerator for at least 30 minutes to completely set the chocolate.

Lift the toffee from the pan by holding the edges of the aluminum foil. Peel the foil away from the toffee and break it into small pieces. Serve at room temperature.

KEEPING: Store the toffee in an airtight container between layers of waxed paper, at room temperature, for up to 2 weeks.

MAKING A CHANGE: Replace the almonds with other nuts or use a combination of nuts. Replace the bittersweet chocolate with dark milk chocolate.

Apricot-Peanut Chocolate Caramel Bars

Makes 15 (1½ x 2¾-inch) bars

These fresh and delectable bars are far better than any store-bought candy bar. That's because they are made with top quality ingredients. A layer of chopped dried apricots and lightly salted peanuts are topped with a layer of caramel then embellished with a layer of dark chocolate. Cut these with a serrated knife so that you can easily cut through the layers. They can be cut into smaller sizes if you like.

Special equipment: 1 (8-inch) square baking pan

Nonstick baking spray
1 cup (8 ounces) coarsely chopped dried apricots
1 cup (5 ounces) skinned, toasted, and lightly salted peanuts
1 recipe Classic Caramel Sauce (page 33), cold
8 ounces semisweet or bittersweet chocolate (56 to 72% cacao content), finely chopped

Line the inside of the baking pan with aluminum foil that hangs over the edges. Spray the inside of the foil with nonstick baking spray.

In a medium bowl, mix the apricots and peanuts together. Turn the mixture out into the lined pan, spreading it evenly into the corners. Evenly spread the caramel sauce over the mixture. Cover tightly with plastic wrap and chill in the refrigerator for 30 minutes to 1 hour.

Melt ¾ of the chocolate in the top of a double boiler over hot water, stirring often, or in a microwave-safe bowl for 30 second bursts, stirring after each burst. Remove the top pan of the double boiler and wipe it completely dry or remove the bowl from the microwave. In 3 stages, stir in the remaining chocolate, making sure each batch is melted before adding the next. Spread the chocolate evenly over the caramel, making sure it reaches into the corners. Cover the pan with aluminum foil and chill in the refrigerator for 30 minutes to 1 hour.

Lift the mixture from the pan with the edges of the aluminum foil then peel the foil gently away. Use a serrated knife to cut into bars, 1½ inches in one direction and 2¾ inches in the other. Serve the bars at room temperature.

KEEPING: Store the bars between layers of waxed paper tightly wrapped in aluminum foil, in the refrigerator, for up to 10 days.

Pistachio Toffee

Makes about 30 pieces

Pistachio nuts are a very popular nut in the Middle East where they are used in both savory dishes and sweets. This candy makes full use of chopped and toasted pistachios by blending them in a cooked buttery toffee and by completely covering the bittersweet chocolate coating with them. The nuts have a light crunchiness and a rather unique, yet enticing, green color. Make sure to thoroughly cover the dipped chocolate candies with the chopped pistachio nuts. If you see that you missed a spot on the chocolate surface just pinch a tiny amount of chopped pistachios on the spot. Because the pistachios have a tendency to crumble off, make sure you serve these candies with plenty of napkins.

Special equipment: candy thermometer and 3 baking sheets

2 tablespoons canola or safflower oil

1^1/$_2$ cups (6 ounces) toasted pistachio nuts, finely chopped, divided

10 tablespoons (5 ounces, 1^1/$_4$ sticks) unsalted butter, cut into small pieces

^{1}/$_2$ cup (3^1/$_2$ ounces) granulated sugar

2 tablespoons water

^{1}/$_4$ teaspoon kosher or fine-grained sea salt

8 ounces bittersweet chocolate (64 to 72% cacao content), finely chopped

Use a paper towel to coat the back of a baking sheet and a pizza wheel with the oil.

Melt the butter in a 3-quart heavy-duty saucepan over medium heat. Add the sugar, water, and salt and cook, stirring constantly, until the mixture registers 260 degrees F on the candy thermometer, about 10 minutes.

Immediately stir in ^{1}/$_4$ cup of the pistachios and continue cooking the mixture until it becomes golden brown and registers 305 degrees F on the thermometer.

Turn the toffee out onto the baking sheet and spread it into a large rectangle. Use the oiled pizza wheel to cut the toffee into pieces that are 1^1/$_2$ inches long and 1 inch wide. Work quickly because the toffee will start to set up. Leave the toffee to cool completely, about 30 minutes.

Use a small offset spatula to lift the pieces of toffee off the back of the baking sheet. Place them onto another baking sheet lined with waxed or parchment paper.

Line another baking sheet with waxed or parchment paper. Place the remaining pistachios in a pie or cake pan.

Melt ¾ of the chocolate in the top of a double boiler over hot water, stirring often, or in a microwave-safe bowl for 30 second bursts, stirring after each burst. Remove the top pan of the double boiler and wipe it completely dry or remove the bowl from the microwave. In 3 stages, stir in the remaining ¼ of the chocolate, making sure each batch is melted before adding the next.

Dip a piece of toffee into the chocolate, coating it completely. With a fork, remove the toffee from the chocolate, gently shake off the excess chocolate, and drop the toffee into the chopped pistachio nuts. Roll the toffee in the pistachios, coating it completely, and place it onto the lined baking sheet. Repeat with the remaining pieces of toffee.

Let the chocolate set up at room temperature or in the refrigerator for about 20 minutes. Serve the toffee at room temperature.

KEEPING: Store the toffee in an airtight container between layers of waxed paper, at room temperature, for up to 2 weeks.

MAKING A CHANGE: Replace the pistachio nuts with other nuts or use a combination of nuts. Replace the bittersweet chocolate with dark milk chocolate.

Caramel Ice Cream

Makes 1 quart

If you are looking for something cold, smooth, and extremely satisfying, this is it. The caramel flavor of this ice cream is intensified by a hint of vanilla and sea salt. Although this ice cream goes well with many other desserts, like cakes and cookies, it easily stands alone.

Special Equipment: candy thermometer and an ice cream maker

2 cups (13 ounces) granulated sugar, divided
¼ cup water
2 cups heavy whipping cream, divided
¼ teaspoon kosher or fine-grained sea salt
4 large egg yolks, room temperature
1 cup milk (whole or 2%)
1 tablespoon pure vanilla extract

Combine 1¼ cups sugar and the water in a 3-quart heavy-duty saucepan. Cook over high heat, without stirring, until the mixture begins to boil. Brush around the inside of the pan with a damp pastry brush at the point where the sugar syrup meets the sides of the pan. Do this twice during the cooking process to prevent the sugar from crystallizing. Continue to cook the mixture, without stirring, until it turns a medium amber color, about 10 minutes.

While the caramel is cooking, heat ¾ cup cream in a small saucepan over medium-high heat and bring to a boil. Stir the hot cream into the caramel, using a long-handle heat-resistant spatula. Be careful because the mixture will bubble and foam. Turn the heat off under the pan. Stir in the salt and blend well.

Whip the egg yolks with the remaining sugar in the bowl of an electric stand mixer using the wire whip attachment, or in a large bowl using a hand-held mixer, until thick and pale and the mixture holds a slowly dissolving ribbon as the beater is lifted, about 5 minutes.

At the same time, heat the milk in a 3-quart heavy-duty saucepan over medium heat until hot. Gradually pour ½ cup of the hot milk into the beaten egg mixture and blend. Then pour this mixture into the saucepan of hot milk. Place the pan over low heat and cook, stirring constantly with a heat-resistant spatula, until the mixture thickens and reaches 185 degrees F on the candy thermometer, 10–15 minutes. At this point, a line drawn through the custard on the back of the spatula should leave a clearly defined path.

continued

Strain the mixture into a large bowl, stir in the remaining cream and vanilla, then add the caramel mixture, and blend together thoroughly. Cover the bowl tightly with plastic wrap to prevent a skin from forming on top and cool to room temperature. Then chill the ice cream mixture in the refrigerator for several hours. Process the mixture in an ice cream maker according to the manufacturer's directions. Be sure to process the ice cream long enough so that it sets up.

KEEPING: Store the ice cream in a tightly covered container in the freezer for 1 month. If it is frozen solid, soften it in the refrigerator for an hour or so before serving.

MAKING A CHANGE: To make Banana Caramel Ice Cream, stir in 1 cup ripe mashed bananas to the ice cream mixture before chilling it. To make Salted Caramel Ice Cream, increase the sea salt to 1 teaspoon. Add 1 cup (4 1/2 ounces) toasted and coarsely chopped walnuts to the ice cream mixture before chilling it.

Coco de Leche Ice Cream

Makes 1 quart

This absolutely delicious, can't-get-enough ice cream has its origins in Latin America, the Caribbean, and Asia. Caramelization is achieved by reducing down a mixture of brown sugar and coconut milk (coco de leche). This ice cream is smooth and creamy, with concentrated coconut flavor that has a subtle roasted aftertaste. As the mixture cooks, it will become light brown in color. Coconut milk can be found in most major supermarkets. Do not use unsweetened, light, or thin coconut milk because it will not caramelize to the required sweetened state.

Special equipment: candy thermometer and an ice cream maker

COCO DULCE DE LECHE

2 cans (13^1/$_2$ ounces each) coconut milk

1^1/$_2$ cups (9 ounces) firmly packed light brown sugar

^{1}/$_2$ teaspoon kosher or fine-grained sea salt

ICE CREAM

1 cup milk (whole or 2%)

2 cups heavy whipping cream

8 large egg yolks, room temperature

^{1}/$_4$ cup (1^1/$_2$ ounces) granulated sugar

GARNISH

2 tablespoons toasted unsweetened coconut

COCO DULCE DE LECHE: Combine the coconut milk, brown sugar, and salt in a 3-quart heavy-duty saucepan. Cook over medium heat to dissolve the sugar. Increase the heat and cook the mixture, stirring occasionally, until it is reduced by a little more than half (yielding 1^3/$_4$ cups), about 40 minutes. Remove the mixture from the heat, transfer to a large bowl, cover the top tightly with plastic wrap, cool to room temperature, then chill in the refrigerator.

ICE CREAM: Place the milk and cream in a 3-quart heavy-duty saucepan. Heat the mixture over medium heat until just below the boiling point

continued

Whip the egg yolks and sugar together in the bowl of an electric stand mixer using the wire whip attachment, or in a large bowl using a hand-held mixer, on high speed until thick and pale and the mixture holds a slowly dissolving ribbon as the beater is lifted, about 5 minutes.

Reduce the mixer speed to low and slowly add 1 cup of the hot cream mixture. Blend well then return the mixture to the saucepan. Place the pan over low heat and cook, stirring constantly with a heat-resistant spatula, until the mixture thickens and reaches 185 degrees F on the candy thermometer, 10–15 minutes. At this point, a line drawn through the custard on the back of the spatula should leave a clearly defined path.

Strain the custard through a fine sieve into a large bowl. Cover tightly and chill in the refrigerator for several hours or overnight.

When you are ready to process the ice cream, stir the Coco de Leche into the ice cream mixture. Process the mixture in an ice cream maker according to the manufacturer's instructions.

Serve scoops of the ice cream sprinkled with the toasted coconut. Or sprinkle chopped nuts on this ice cream, such as toasted macadamias or almonds.

KEEPING: Store the ice cream in a covered container in the freezer for up to 1 month. If it is frozen solid, soften it in the refrigerator for an hour or so before serving.

STREAMLINING: The Coco Dulce de Leche can be made up to a week in advance. Store it tightly covered with plastic wrap in the refrigerator.

Caramel Crunch Ice Cream

Makes 1 quart

Vanilla and caramel are natural flavor partners. This smooth and velvety vanilla bean ice cream gets its flavor boost from small caramel shards. The crunchy caramel shards provide an exciting mouth feel as they release yummy caramel flavor. Although the caramel pieces may seem like they have sharp edges when you break and chop the cooled mixture, these edges will smooth out, and even shrink a little, during the processing of the ice cream mixture. You can substitute vanilla bean paste for the vanilla beans in this recipe.

Special equipment: candy thermometer, a jelly roll pan, and an ice cream maker

ICE CREAM
2 cups milk (whole or 2%)
2 cups heavy whipping cream
5 vanilla beans
8 large egg yolks, room temperature
3/4 cup (5 ounces) granulated sugar

CARAMEL SHARDS
2 cups (13 ounces) granulated sugar
1/2 cup water
1/2 teaspoon cream of tartar

ICE CREAM: Place the milk and cream in a 3-quart heavy-duty saucepan. Using a sharp knife, split the vanilla beans lengthwise. Scrape out the seeds and add the beans and seeds to the liquid. Heat the mixture over medium heat until just below the boiling point. Remove from the heat, cover, and let the mixture infuse for 30 minutes.

Whip the egg yolks and sugar together in the bowl of an electric stand mixer using the wire whip attachment, or in a large bowl using a hand-held mixer, on high speed until thick and pale and the mixture holds a slowly dissolving ribbon as the beater is lifted, about 5 minutes.

Meanwhile, reheat the cream mixture to just below boiling. Reduce the mixer speed to low and slowly add 1 cup of the hot cream mixture. Blend well then pour the mixture into the saucepan. Place the pan over low heat and cook, stirring constantly with a heat-resistant spatula, until the mixture thickens and reaches 185 degrees F on the candy thermometer, 10–15 minutes. At this point, a line drawn through the custard on the back of the spatula should leave a clearly defined path.

Strain the custard through fine sieve into a large bowl. Cover tightly and chill in the refrigerator for several hours or overnight.

CARAMEL SHARDS: Line the jelly roll pan with a nonstick silicone mat.

Combine the sugar, water, and cream of tartar in a 3-quart heavy-duty saucepan. When mixture comes to a boil, brush around the inside of the pan with a damp pastry brush at the point where the sugar syrup meets the sides of the pan. Do this twice during the cooking process to prevent the sugar from crystallizing. Cook over high heat, without stirring, until it is a medium amber color, about 9 minutes.

Remove the pan from the heat, pour the mixture onto the jelly roll pan, and spread it out with a spatula. Work quickly because the mixture sets up rapidly.

Let the caramel cool completely, about 30 minutes, then break it into small pieces with your hands. It may be necessary to chop some of the pieces smaller using a chefs' knife on a cutting board. The pieces should be about ½-inch.

When you are ready to process the ice cream, stir the caramel shards into the ice cream mixture. Process the mixture in an ice cream maker according to the manufacturer's instructions.

KEEPING: Store the caramel shards between layers of waxed paper in a tightly covered container, at room temperature, for up to 1 week.

Store the ice cream in a covered container in the freezer for up to 1 month. If it is frozen solid, soften it in the refrigerator for an hour or so before serving.

Caramelized White Chocolate Ice Cream

Makes 1¹/₂ quarts

The flavor emphasis in this ice cream is white chocolate with subtle caramel overtones, a delightful and rewarding flavor combination. The ice cream has a smooth and creamy mouth feel with a slight caramel color. It is an excellent partner for another caramel ice cream or two, and my favorite caramel cookie with this is Hazelnut Praline Biscotti (page 125).

Special equipment: candy thermometer and an ice cream maker

1 cup Caramelized White Chocolate (page 35)
1 cup milk (whole or 2%)
2 cups heavy whipping cream
1 teaspoon pure vanilla bean paste or pure vanilla extract
6 large egg yolks, room temperature
²/₃ cup (4 ounces) superfine sugar

Place the Caramelized White Chocolate in a large bowl. If it is firm, soften it in a microwave oven on low power for 30 second bursts, stirring between each burst.

Place the milk and cream in a 3-quart heavy-duty saucepan. Add the vanilla bean paste and stir to combine. Bring the mixture to a simmer over medium heat.

Whip the egg yolks and sugar in the bowl of an electric stand mixer using the wire whip attachment, or in a large bowl using a hand-held mixer, until thick and pale and the mixture holds a slowly dissolving ribbon as the beater is lifted, about 5 minutes.

Ladle half of the hot milk mixture into a liquid measuring cup and pour slowly into the egg yolk mixture to temper the yolks. Pour this mixture back into the saucepan. Stir the mixture constantly until it is thick enough to coat the spoon or registers 185 degrees F on the candy thermometer. Immediately remove the thermometer and place it in a glass of warm water. Strain the mixture into the bowl of Caramelized White Chocolate.

Stir to completely blend the mixture. Cover the bowl tightly with plastic wrap, place on a cooling rack, and cool to room temperature. Chill in the refrigerator for several hours. Process the ice cream in an ice cream maker following the manufacturer's instructions.

KEEPING: Store the ice cream in a tightly covered container in the freezer for up to 2 weeks. If it is frozen solid, soften it in the refrigerator for an hour or so before serving.

STREAMLINING: The ice cream custard can be made up to 3 days in advance and kept tightly covered in a bowl in the refrigerator before freezing in the ice cream maker.

MAKING A CHANGE: To make Caramelized Milk Chocolate Ice Cream, replace the Caramelized White Chocolate with Caramelized Milk Chocolate (page 35).

ADDING STYLE: Serve scoops of the ice cream with fresh raspberries or blueberries.

Salted Caramel Dark Chocolate Chunk Ice Cream

Makes 1 quart

Sea salt helps bring forward the rich caramel flavor and the dark chocolate chunks add an extra complimentary flavor prize. I like to include a scoop of this ice cream alongside a piece of cake or tart. And any time of year is good for this ice cream.

Special equipment: candy thermometer and an ice cream maker

1¹/₂ cups (10 ounces) granulated sugar, divided

¹/₄ cup water

1 tablespoon light corn syrup

2 cups heavy whipping cream

2 cups milk (whole or 2%)

1 teaspoon sea salt

6 large egg yolks, room temperature

6 ounces bittersweet chocolate (66 to 72% cacao content), chopped into very small chunks

Combine 1 cup sugar, the water, and corn syrup in a 3-quart heavy-duty saucepan. Cook over high heat, without stirring, until the mixture begins to boil. Brush around the inside of the pan with a damp pastry brush at the point where the sugar syrup meets the sides of the pan. Do this twice during the cooking process to prevent the sugar from crystallizing. Continue to cook the mixture, without stirring, until it turns a medium amber color, about 10 minutes.

While the caramel is cooking, combine the cream and milk in a 2-quart saucepan over medium heat and bring to a simmer.

Turn off the heat under the pan of the caramel mixture. Stir the hot cream mixture into the caramel, using a long-handle heat-resistant spatula. Be careful because the mixture will bubble and foam. Stir in the sea salt and blend well.

continued

Whisk the egg yolks with the remaining sugar in a medium bowl. Pour 1 cup of the hot caramel mixture into the egg yolks and stir together. Then pour this mixture into the saucepan with the caramel mixture. Place over medium heat and cook, stirring constantly with a heat-resistant spatula, until the mixture thickens and reaches 185 degrees F on the candy thermometer, 10–15 minutes. At this point, a line drawn through the custard on the back of the spatula should leave a clearly defined path.

Strain the mixture into a large bowl, cover with plastic wrap to prevent a skin from forming on top, and cool to room temperature. Chill the ice cream mixture in the refrigerator for several hours. Process the mixture in an ice cream maker according to the manufacturer's directions. After 15 minutes of processing, add the chocolate chunks to the ice cream. Be sure to process the ice cream long enough so that it sets up.

KEEPING: Store the ice cream in a tightly covered container in the freezer for 1 month. If it is frozen solid, soften it in the refrigerator for an hour or so before serving.

MAKING A CHANGE: Replace the dark chocolate chunks with milk chocolate chunks.

Caramel Ice Cream Sundae

Makes 4 sundaes

This is my nomination for the world's best sundae. Creamy caramel ice cream is drizzled with bittersweet chocolate sauce that is sprinkled with toasted chopped walnuts. One of the best things about this sundae is that everything can be prepared in advance, except for the need to warm the sauce. If you want to be a little creative, other chopped nuts can be used to top off this "world's best sundae."

Special equipment: 4 sundae bowls or glasses

BITTERSWEET CHOCOLATE SAUCE

1/2 cup (3 ounces) firmly packed light brown sugar

3/4 cup heavy whipping cream

1 teaspoon pure vanilla extract

Pinch of kosher or fine-grained sea salt

6 ounces bittersweet chocolate (66% to 72% cacao content), finely chopped

3 tablespoons (1 1/2 ounces) unsalted butter, softened

SUNDAES

1 quart Caramel Ice Cream (page 187)

1/4 cup (1 ounce) toasted walnuts, coarsely chopped

BITTERSWEET CHOCOLATE SAUCE: In a 2-quart heavy-duty saucepan, combine the brown sugar, cream, vanilla, and salt. Stir frequently to dissolve the sugar then bring to a simmer over medium heat.

Remove the pan from the heat and stir in the chocolate and butter until completely melted and smooth.

Use the sauce immediately or transfer to a bowl, cover with plastic wrap, and cool on a rack to room temperature. Warm the sauce in the top of a double boiler or in a microwave oven on low power before using.

SUNDAES: Place 2 scoops of Caramel Ice Cream in each sundae bowl and drizzle Bittersweet Chocolate Sauce over them. Repeat with 1 more scoop of ice cream and more chocolate sauce. Sprinkle the top of each sundae with the walnuts. Serve immediately.

KEEPING: Store the sauce in a tightly covered container in the refrigerator for up to a week.

MAKING A CHANGE: Replace one of the scoops of Caramel Ice Cream with vanilla ice cream. Replace the walnuts with toasted, skinned, and finely chopped hazelnuts.

Other Caramel Desserts

Caramel Apple Crisp

Makes 9 servings

Rich caramelized apple filling takes this all-American favorite to the next level. The traditional topping with rolled oats and spices is a perfect partner with the caramelized apple filling. During baking, the sugar that is in the topping caramelizes creating a slight crunchiness. To avoid the filling being too runny, allow the crisp to cool for a short while before cutting.

Special equipment: 1 (8-inch) square baking pan

TOPPING

$1/2$ cup ($2 1/4$ ounces) all-purpose flour
$1/3$ cup ($1 1/2$ ounces) old-fashioned rolled oats
$1/2$ cup ($3 1/2$ ounces) granulated sugar
$1/2$ teaspoon ground cinnamon
$1/4$ teaspoon kosher or fine-grained sea salt
$1/8$ teaspoon freshly grated nutmeg
6 tablespoons (3 ounces, $3/4$ stick) unsalted butter, chilled

CARAMEL APPLE FILLING

4 medium Granny Smith or Pippin apples
$1/2$ cup ($3 1/2$ ounces) granulated sugar
4 tablespoons (2 ounces, $1/2$ stick) unsalted butter, cut into small pieces
1 tablespoon freshly squeezed lemon juice
$1/4$ teaspoon kosher or fine-grained sea salt

TOPPING: Briefly pulse together the flour, oats, sugar, cinnamon, salt, and nutmeg in the work bowl of a food processor fitted with the steel blade. Cut the butter into small pieces and add. Pulse until the butter is cut into tiny pieces. Transfer the mixture to a small bowl, cover tightly with plastic wrap, and chill in the refrigerator until ready to use.

CARAMEL APPLE FILLING: Peel, quarter, and core the apples. Cut each quarter into 3 pieces, lengthwise. Place the apple slices in a large bowl.

Position a rack in the center of the oven and preheat to 375 degrees F.

continued

Combine the sugar and butter together in a large sauté pan. Cook over medium heat until the butter is completely melted and the mixture is smooth. Add the lemon juice and cook, stirring frequently, until the mixture turns deep amber colored. Add the salt and then the apples. Stir until the apples are completely coated with the caramel, about 2 minutes.

Transfer the mixture to the baking pan. Sprinkle the topping evenly over the apple mixture. Bake the crisp for 50 minutes, or until the topping is light golden and the sauce bubbles. Remove the baking pan from the oven and transfer to a cooling rack, for 15–20 minutes. Serve scoops of the warm crisp.

KEEPING: The crisp can be kept tightly covered with aluminum foil, at room temperature, for up to 2 days. Warm it in a 350 degree F oven for 15 minutes before serving.

ADDING STYLE: Accompany each serving of the crisp with a scoop of nonfat Greek-style yogurt or lightly whipped cream.

Banana-Strawberry Caramel Napoleons

Makes 4 napoleons

This dessert looks as good as it tastes. It's a variation of the classic French Napoleon—that pastry that always catches your eye in pastry shops. Three airy layers of puff pastry are sandwiched with fresh sliced bananas, strawberries, and light fluffy caramel whipped cream. This is made with frozen puff pastry which is easy to work with and tastes great. Although one of these Napoleons can easily satisfy two people, the recipe can be doubled to make more.

Special equipment: 1 baking sheet

1 sheet store-bought frozen puff pastry, thawed
2/3 cup heavy whipping cream
1 tablespoon confectioners' sugar, sifted
1/2 cup Classic Caramel Sauce (page 33)
1 medium banana, thinly sliced
4 medium strawberries, thinly sliced

Position a rack in the center of the oven and preheat to 400 degrees F. Line the baking sheet with parchment paper or a nonstick liner.

Unfold the sheet of puff pastry and cut into 6 equal-size rectangles. Place the rectangles on the baking sheet and bake for 12–15 minutes, until puffed and golden colored. Remove the baking sheet from the oven and cool completely on a rack.

Whip the cream and sugar in the bowl of an electric stand mixer using the wire whip attachment, or in a mixing bowl using a hand-held mixer, until firm but not stiff peaks. Fold the caramel sauce into the whipped cream until completely blended.

Cut each puff pastry rectangle in half across the width. Choose 4 pieces of puff pastry for the bottoms. Using 1/4 of the whipped cream mixture, spread each of the bottoms with a thin layer. Place banana slices on the whipped cream and spread them with another 1/4 of the whipped cream.

continued

Place a second layer of puff pastry on top of the cream mixture and spread it with another ¼ of the whipped cream. Arrange the cut strawberries on the cream and spread with the remaining whipped cream. Place the third layer of puff pastry on top and press together gently.

Serve the napoleons immediately or store in the refrigerator no longer than 3 hours. If serving them from the refrigerator, let them sit for 10 minutes before serving so they will be cool but not cold.

KEEPING: The napoleons will keep tightly covered with plastic wrap in the refrigerator up to 3 hours before serving.

STREAMLINING: The puff pastry can be baked 1 day in advance of assembling the napoleons. Store tightly covered with aluminum foil at room temperature.

MAKING A CHANGE: Use all strawberries or bananas or other fresh fruit that you like, such as other berries, kiwi, or mango.

Caramel Cream Puffs

Makes 15 cream puffs

These classic cream puffs are filled with smooth and light Caramel-Honey Whipped Cream. The caramel and honey combination offers a sweet, but not overly sweet, flavor that tastes exactly as you would expect, like caramel honey. The cream puffs can be made a couple of days in advance and then filled before serving.

Special equipment: 1 (12-inch) pastry bag, 1 (^{1}/2-inch) open plain round pastry tip, 1 large open star tip, and 2 baking sheets

CARAMEL-HONEY WHIPPED CREAM

1^1/4 cups heavy whipping cream

^{2}/3 cup (4 ounces) granulated sugar

3 tablespoons water

^{1}/4 teaspoon cream of tartar

^{1}/2 teaspoon pure vanilla extract

1 tablespoon honey

CREAM PUFFS

^{1}/2 cup water

4 tablespoons (2 ounces, ^{1}/2 stick) unsalted butter, cut into small pieces

2 tablespoons superfine sugar

Pinch of kosher or fine-grained sea salt

^{1}/2 cup (2^1/4 ounces) all-purpose flour

2 large eggs, room temperature

GARNISH

1 large egg, room temperature

1 teaspoon milk

ASSEMBLY

Confectioners' sugar

CARAMEL-HONEY WHIPPED CREAM: Bring the cream to a boil in a 1-quart saucepan over medium heat. Cook the sugar, water, and cream of tartar in a 2-quart heavy-duty saucepan over high heat until the mixture comes to a boil. Brush around the inside of the pan with a damp pastry brush at the point where the sugar syrup meets

continued

the sides of the pan. Do this twice during the cooking process to prevent the sugar from crystallizing. Cook the mixture over high heat, without stirring, until it turns amber colored, 6–8 minutes.

Lower the heat to medium and slowly add the hot cream to the sugar mixture while stirring constantly. The cream will bubble and foam. Continue to stir to make sure there are no lumps. Remove the saucepan from the heat and stir in the vanilla.

Transfer the mixture to a large bowl, cover tightly with plastic wrap, and cool to room temperature. Chill in the refrigerator at least 3 hours or overnight.

CREAM PUFFS: Position a rack in the center of the oven and preheat to 400 degrees F. Line a baking sheet with parchment paper or a nonstick liner.

Combine the water, butter, sugar, and salt in a 2-quart heavy-duty saucepan and bring to a boil over medium-high heat. Add the flour and stir vigorously with a heat-resistant spatula until the flour is completely mixed in, 1–2 minutes. The mixture will form a ball around the spatula.

Remove the saucepan from the heat and transfer the mixture to the bowl of an electric stand mixer or a medium bowl. Using the flat beater attachment or a hand-held mixer, beat the mixture on medium speed until steam stops rising from it, about 4 minutes. Add the eggs, 1 at a time, mixing well after each addition, and stop frequently to scrape down the sides of the bowl with a rubber spatula. Beat for another 1–2 minutes, until the mixture is smooth.

Fit the pastry bag with the plain round tip and fill the pastry bag partway with the cream puff pastry. Hold the pastry bag 1 inch above a baking sheet and pipe out 2-inch mounds, leaving 2 inches of space between them.

GARNISH: In a small bowl, lightly beat together the egg and milk. Brush the tops of the cream puffs with the egg wash.

Bake the cream puffs 25–30 minutes, or until golden and firm. Check one cream puff by splitting it open. If it is still damp inside, bake the puffs another 3–5 minutes, until dry. Transfer the baking sheets to racks to cool completely.

ASSEMBLY: Slice each cream puff open horizontally. Place the caramel cream in the bowl of an electric stand mixer or a mixing bowl. Add the honey. Use a wire whip attachment or a hand-held mixer to whip the cream on medium-high speed until it holds soft peaks.

Fit the pastry bag with the star tip and fill the pastry bag partway with the mixture. Pipe the filling into the bottom halves of the cream puffs, filling each. Place the tops of the cream puffs on top of the filling. Lightly dust the tops of the cream puffs with confectioners' sugar and serve at room temperature.

KEEPING: Store the unfilled cream puffs, at room temperature, covered with aluminum foil for up to 2 days, or freeze in a freezer-safe container for up to 4 months. If frozen, defrost in the refrigerator overnight before filling.

The filled cream puffs can be kept covered in the refrigerator for 3–4 hours before serving.

STREAMLINING: The Caramel-Honey Whipped Cream can be kept in a tightly covered container in the refrigerator for up to 3 days before whipping.

ADDING STYLE: Serve the cream puffs with Classic Caramel Sauce (page 33).

Bread Pudding with Caramel Sauce

Makes 8 to 10 servings

This cozy dessert may remind you of something your mother or grandmother used to make. The bread, cream, sugars, and walnut mixture is spiced up with small amounts of vanilla and nutmeg. This is all topped off with scrumptious Classic Caramel Sauce. In addition to reheating this dessert, it can be served at room temperature or cool right out of the refrigerator.

Special equipment: 1 (2-quart) baking dish and 1 baking sheet

TO PREPARE THE BAKING DISH

1 tablespoon unsalted butter, softened

1 tablespoon granulated sugar

BREAD PUDDING

1 cup (4^1/2 ounces) coarsely chopped walnuts

^{3}/4 fresh or day-old baguette or ^{1}/2 loaf fresh or day-old good quality white bread

1 cup milk

2 cups heavy whipping cream

5 large eggs, room temperature

2 teaspoons pure vanilla extract

^{1}/2 cup (3^1/2 ounces) granulated sugar

^{1}/2 cup (3 ounces) firmly packed light brown sugar

^{1}/4 teaspoon kosher or fine-grained sea salt

^{1}/4 teaspoon freshly grated nutmeg

Boiling water

^{1}/2 cup Classic Caramel Sauce (page 33), room temperature

TO PREPARE THE BAKING DISH: Use a paper towel or your fingertips to coat the inside of the baking dish with the butter. Sprinkle with the sugar.

Position a rack in the center of the oven and preheat to 350 degrees F. Place the walnuts in a cake or pie pan and toast in the oven for 8 minutes. Remove the pan from the oven and cool on a rack. Adjust the oven heat to 400 degrees F.

Cut the crusts off the bread and cut the bread into 1-inch cubes. Place the cubes in a shallow layer on the baking sheet and dry in the oven for 15 minutes. Transfer the dry bread cubes to the baking dish and sprinkle them with the toasted walnuts.

In a large bowl, whisk together the milk, cream, eggs, vanilla, sugars, salt, and nutmeg and blend thoroughly.

Pour this mixture over the bread and walnuts in the baking dish. Cover the dish tightly with plastic wrap and place in the refrigerator for 30 minutes. This gives the bread time to soak up the liquid. Adjust the oven heat to 350 degrees F.

Remove the plastic from the baking dish. Place the bread pudding dish in a larger baking pan. Place the baking pan on the oven rack and pour the water halfway up the sides of the dish. Bake for 35–45 minutes, or until the pudding is puffed and a cake tester or toothpick inserted in the center comes out clean.

Remove the baking pan from the oven. Remove the bread pudding from the water bath and cool for 15 minutes on a rack. Drizzle the caramel sauce evenly over the top of the bread pudding. Serve scoops of the bread pudding while warm.

KEEPING: Store the bread pudding tightly covered with plastic wrap in the refrigerator for up to 3 days.

Warm the bread pudding in a 350 degrees F oven for 15 minutes before serving.

Caramelized Roasted Pears

Makes 8 servings

This very simple to prepare dessert is all about the fresh fruit flavor of pears that is amplified by caramelizing them. To top off the caramelized pears, each half pear is garnished with vivid and smooth Caramel-Honey Whipped Cream. I like to use Bosc pears, but you can use any type of pears for this dessert.

Special equipment: 1 large roasting pan

6 tablespoons (3 ounces, $^3/_4$ stick) unsalted butter, melted
1$^1/_2$ cups (9 ounces) firmly packed light brown sugar
4 medium pears (about 2 pounds)
$^1/_2$ recipe Caramel-Honey Whipped Cream (page 210), optional

Position a rack in the center of the oven and preheat to 400 degrees F. Place the butter in the roasting pan and stir in the brown sugar.

Cut the pears in half lengthwise and remove the core using a melon baller. Leave the stems intact, if possible.

Place the pears, cut side down, on top of the butter mixture. Bake for 30 minutes. Remove the pan from the oven, turn the pears over, so the cut side faces up, and baste with the caramel mixture. Bake for another 10 minutes, until the pears are golden.

Remove the pan from the oven and cool slightly. Serve the pears on dessert plates or in bowls and garnish each with a dollop of Caramel-Honey Whipped cream, if desired.

KEEPING: The pears are best served the day they are made. Hold them at room temperature covered with aluminum foil. They can be rewarmed in a 350 degrees F oven for 10–15 minutes.

Sources

Amano Artisan Chocolate
www.amanochocolate.com
801.655.1996
Amano makes a variety of outstanding single origin 70 percent cacao chocolates and single origin dark milk chocolate.

E. Guittard Chocolate
www.guittard.com
800.468.2462
E. Guittard artisan chocolates are single origin and offer unique flavors. They are available through the website as well as at several cookware shops and gourmet markets throughout the United States.

JB Prince Company
www.jbprince.com
800.473.0577
JB Prince carries a large selection of baking and pastry making equipment.

King Arthur Flour
www.kingarthurflour.com
800.827.6836
King Arthur Flour's online shop carries a large variety of equipment and ingredients.

Pastry Chef Central
www.pastrychef.com
561.999.9483
Pastry Chef Central carries professional grade baking equipment, tools, and ingredients.

Scharffen Berger Chocolate Maker
www.scharffenberger.com
866.608.6944
Scharffen Berger makes high-quality dark chocolate in various cacao percentages, as well as dark milk chocolate, available through their website and at many cookware and grocery shops throughout the United States.

Sur La Table
www.surlatable.com
800.243.0852
Sur La Table carries a large variety of equipment and tools available at their many stores throughout the United States, as well as online.

The Cook's Warehouse
www.cookswarehouse.com
866.890.5962
The Cook's Warehouse carries a wide variety of equipment and tools available at their four locations in Atlanta and online.

Williams-Sonoma
www.williams-sonoma.com
877.812.6235
Williams-Sonoma stocks a wide variety of equipment and some ingredients at their stores throughout the United States, as well as online.

Measurement Equivalents

U.S. MEASURING SYSTEM	METRIC SYSTEM
CAPACITY	**APPROXIMATE CAPACITY**
¼ teaspoon	1.25 milliliters
1 teaspoon	5 milliliters
1 tablespoon	15 milliliters
¼ cup	60 milliliters
1 cup (8 fluid ounces)	240 milliliters
2 cups (1 pint; 16 fluid ounces)	470 milliliters
4 cups (1 quart; 32 fluid ounces)	0.95 liter
4 quarts (1 gallon; 64 fluid ounces)	3.78 liters

U.S. MEASURING SYSTEM	METRIC SYSTEM
WEIGHT	**APPROXIMATE WEIGHT**
1 dry ounce	15 grams
2 ounces	30 grams
4 ounces (¼ pound)	110 grams
8 ounces (½ pound)	230 grams
16 ounces (1 pound)	454 grams

LIQUID MEASUREMENT

MEASUREMENT	FLUID OUNCES	OUNCES BY WEIGHT	GRAMS
2 tablespoons	1 fluid ounce	½ ounce	14 grams
¼ cup	2 fluid ounces	1¾ ounces	50 grams
⅓ cup	2⅔ fluid ounces	2 ounces	70 grams
½ cup	4 fluid ounces	4 ounces	113 grams
⅔ cup	5⅓ fluid ounces	5 ounces	142 grams
¾ cup	6 fluid ounces	5¼ ounces	177 grams
1 cup	8 fluid ounces	8 ounces	227 grams

LIQUID MEASUREMENT

MEASUREMENT	EQUIVALENT
¼ cup (2 fluid ounces)	5 tablespoons
⅓ cup (2⅔ fluid ounces)	7 tablespoons
½ cup (4 fluid ounces)	11 tablespoons
⅔ cup (5⅓ fluid ounces)	14 tablespoons
¾ cup (6 fluid ounces)	16 tablespoons
1 cup (8 fluid ounces)	20 tablespoons

DRY MEASUREMENT

MEASUREMENT	EQUIVALENT
3 teaspoons	1 tablespoon
2 tablespoons	⅛ cup
4 tablespoons	¼ cup
5⅓ tablespoons	⅓ cup
8 tablespoons	½ cup
10⅔ tablespoons	⅔ cup
12 tablespoons	¾ cup
16 tablespoons	1 cup

Index

About the Author

Carole Bloom is a European-trained pastry chef and confectioner who has worked in five-star hotels and restaurants in Europe and the United States. She is the award-winning author of ten other cookbooks, including *Intensely Chocolate, Bite-Size Desserts, The Essential Baker,* and *Truffles, Candies, and Confections.* Her articles and recipes have appeared in *Bon Appétit, Chocolatier, Cooking Light, Cooking Smart, Eating Well, Fine Cooking, Food and Wine, Gourmet,* online at Epicurious.com and at Culinate.com. Carole has been a national spokesperson for chocolate groups and associations, as well as a celebrity judge and spokesperson for Sam's Club. She has made many television appearances including The Today Show, ABC World News This Morning, and CNN. She is also a frequent-featured speaker at international culinary conferences and trade shows. Carole teaches dessert classes at cooking schools throughout the country.

Carole is a Certified Culinary Professional (CCP) by the International Association of Culinary Professionals (IACP). She holds a Bachelor of Arts degree in Fine Arts from the University of California, at Berkeley. She is also a certified yoga teacher, registered with Yoga Alliance (RYT). Carole lives in Carlsbad, California, with her husband and their pampered cat. Please visit her website at www.carolebloom.com.